IAN SMITH

FIND YOUR HILL

(WORTH FIGHTING FOR)

Identifiers: ISBN   979-8-2182030-0-9

Find YOUR Hill. Copyright 2022 by Ian Smith

Library of Congress Cataloging – in Publication Data

Names: Smith, Ian, author

Title: Find YOUR Hill

Description: First Edition

First Edition: 2023

Published by Thrive Publishing

1100 Suite #100 Riverwalk Terrace

Jenks, OK 74037

TABLE OF CONTENTS

FOREWORD

BY ANDY FRISELLA

America was founded by farmers, merchants, businessmen, scholars, and warriors. They were regular people who desired to be free – free to do their business and live their lives without the oppression and interference of tyrants thousands of miles away. Brave people.

In March 2020 when it was decided that for the first time in history, the government was shutting down businesses for the pandemic, I knew it would be disastrous for small and medium-sized businesses. I have been an entrepreneur my entire life and understand how hard it is to keep a business open in regular times, much less in a forced shutdown. I knew we were in deep shit. I have been in business for well over 20 years and ran through multiple pandemics, shutting down the economy was not standard protocol. The social pressure to comply with these lockdowns was enormous. There were very few people resisting the shutdown and calling bullshit on what was happening because of the insane amount of fear and propaganda put in front of our eyes and in our ears 24 hours a day. The videos of people falling over in the street of China, and death counters on every news channel, it was panic and hysteria from every direction.

It was scary... at first.

Shutting down the economy and closing small businesses while "essential businesses" stayed open was a major red flag. Never in the history of this country has the government stepped in and told small businesses to close while allowing major corporations in the world to absorb the market. It was not hard for me to catch on to what they were doing. I started to speak out and was met with nearly 100% resistance. The attacks were vile, disgusting, and personal. I was immediately labeled a conspiracy theorist and a dancer for society for pointing out what I saw to be wrong. I was harassed, "cancelled" many times, and had a man break into my house and paint "welcome to the no-fly list" on my walls in red paint.

I was in the fight.

The groupthink and hysteria were at levels that I had never seen in my life, and I felt very alone. There were a few people who agreed with me, but not many. The ones who agreed did so quietly in private messages. Most of the people I knew, even those closest to me, questioned me in private, but I knew this was wrong and there was much more to it all than what was understood by most.

I understood clearly that this move would permanently shut down many small businesses across the country. Most people do not understand that many small businesses are a bad month or two away from being out of business, even in great times. That is just the reality of the business, it is not for the faint of heart. I could not see how these restaurants, gyms, and other small businesses were going to survive. I knew that people had to immediately fight to stay open, but I did not see many fighting.

I saw one though. While scrolling through my phone on Instagram at the end of the day, I came across this dude with a long beard. His post had been shared by a mutual friend that I trusted. I took some time to read the caption on his post. That man was Ian Smith, little did I know that this dude, whom I had never seen before, would become a brother to me, and one of the men I respect and love most.

The caption told the story of Ian standing up and keeping his gym open in defiance of the lockdowns in New Jersey. I immediately recognized that what he was doing was the start of something massive. I messaged him to share my sentiments. I remember telling him that what he was doing was extremely important to the future of freedom in this country, to keep going, and to let me know how I could help his efforts. At that time, I had no idea how important that message would become.

Almost immediately, we began speaking daily. We still do. We vent frustrations, strategize, and find ways to drive courage into the hearts of others to join the fight to resist what we both saw then – and most see now – as tyrannical government overreach.

Over the course of the last three years, I have learned a lot about our country, our people, and Ian Smith. Let me be the first to tell you that not a single thing about Ian is perfect. Just like there is not one part of me or you that is perfect, but that is exactly who this country was founded by. Imperfect people with hope and courage to make a better life. Courageous people. Brave people. People who were willing to fight for what they believed in. People who are willing to stand up to wrong, even when it is hard to do so. That is what I see when I look at Ian Smith. He possesses the kind of courage that the men who founded this country had. When I look at Ian, I see the spirit of those men inside him. I can feel it.

What he has, everyone needs right now.

Ian is a regular American man who embodies the qualities that our founders had. The ability to stand virtually alone and draw a line in the sand in the face of the biggest, most powerful government in the world. If everyone had this, we would not be in the current predicament our country is in.

If you take a good look at our Constitution, it does not take long to see that the America we have today, and America outlined in that document is not in alignment. Not even close. Our country is over-taxed, over-litigated, over-regulated, and riddled with violent crime. Everywhere we look we see poverty, homelessness, and major corruption at all levels of government. We are being pushed into racial division and political polarization and told we must accept the sexualization of children in the name of inclusion and tolerance. We are being manipulated by the collusion of Big Tech, Government, Big Business, Mainstream Media, and Hollywood 24 hours a day. We are told this is normal, and it is not. This is not how this country is supposed to be. This is not acceptable.

We, as Americans, deserve better.

We, as citizens of the world, deserve better.

...but it takes courage to make it better.

If we all had the courage of Ian Smith...

If we all valued freedom the way he does...

If we were all willing to stand up and say NO...

None of the hardships our country currently faces would exist.

That is what I want you to take away from this book.

You do not need a platform.

You do not need to be a celebrity.

You do not need to be someone everyone knows and recognizes.

In fact, you are exactly who you need to be...

...but you need to Find Your Hill and fight on it.

I could write an entire book about who Ian is, and what he means to me. This book is not about Ian.

This book is about you.

So, when you read about the life of this incredible man, one of my absolute best friends, see yourself in his story:

Ask yourself, what is this country worth to you?

What is your freedom worth to you?

Will you acknowledge your own power and influence in creating a world you are proud to be a part of?

Will you hand down to future generations the freedoms that allow you the opportunities to live an exceptional life?

The men and women who founded this country nearly two-hundred-fifty years ago asked themselves some of those same questions. Not only did they think about it, but they also found their hill and fought on it with all they had. Everything that you have known and loved about America came from those people. Everything.

Will you be a part of the generation that lets this country fail, Or will you be a part of the generation that saves it?

Ian made his choice a long time ago and so did I, along with many other brave Americans. I hope this book will help you make the same choice.

Everything depends on it.

Andy Frisella

Regular Dude CEO

This story is dedicated to my son, Ian Jr.
The world is yours, kid.

I LOVE YOU

ENDORSEMENTS

"I get a lot of emails on my show, no matter what I talk about there are always haters, I received over 500 emails about the show Ian was on, every single one of them supported what he was doing. He did the right thing!"

DAN BONGINO (RET. SECRET SERVICE, FOX NEWS)

"I remember when I first heard of a gym owner in NJ that kept his gym open despite facing enormous pressure from the state government. I remember thinking how rare it is to find someone with the courage to take a leap of faith and do the right thing, despite not necessarily knowing about the outcome or maybe even caring about the negative secondary effects to oneself personally. There are few men in this world like that. Ian Smith is one of the most courageous people I've ever seen from afar, although as a fellow New Jerseyan, I feel a special kinship with a person from my state who fights. In a country that so predicated on fear of fear, meeting Ian in New York at the 2021 NYC Young Republican Gala was refreshing. He's one of only a few people I've ever met that I asked for a picture with!"

JAMES OKEEFE (FOUNDER PROJECT VERITAS, CEO O'KEEFE MEDIA GROUP)

"Ian is a warrior! When most wilted to unconstitutional lockdowns, Ian and the gym defied cowardly groupthink and inspired a nation. They are the definition of free citizens fighting back the right way. We'd better learn from Ian and his courageous leadership — or we will lose our freedoms."

PETE HEGSETH (FOX NEWS, RET. NAVY SEAL)

"I fully endorsed Ian Smith to run for Congress. He is exactly the kind of guy who needs to be in a leadership position in our Government. Ian Smith stood up for this country."

GEN M. FLYNN (RET. US ARMY LT. GENERAL)

INTRODUCTION

> "The power of storytelling is exactly
> this: to bridge the gaps where
> everything else has crumbled."
> **— Paulo Coelho**

Writing a book about yourself is a challenging task. It is easy to sound like an asshole. Nobody wants to read two hundred pages of "I did this…" then "I did that…" and "I said this…" I know I sure would not.

My goal in writing this book is not to tell you about myself, but to tell you my story and what I have learned through those experiences. In the end, the purpose is for you to see yourself in the narrative and to walk away empowered, with a sense of purpose.

There have been many times in my life when I have felt powerless and lost. Life has taught me that I was wrong about my insignificance.

This book was plagued with difficulty and hurdles along the way. The idea to tell this story started two years ago, and there were many times when I was ready to scrap it. I doubted myself and the importance of sharing my experiences. Who am I to write an autobiography? I appreciate the patience that people have afforded me, it means the world that after two years of waiting, people still want to hear what I have to say.

I hope you read this book and understand how important you are. I hope you realize how powerful you are. I hope you realize how needed you are. I hope you make your mark on the world. I hope you enjoy the story and laugh as much as you learn through the chapters ahead.

Let's dig in.

CHAPTER 1:

DARKEST HOUR

"Honor and shame from no condition rise. Act
well your part: there all the honor lies."
- **Alexander Pope**

THE NIGHTMARE.

I hear the music skipping.

I taste blood.

I see my shattered windshield.

I can feel chipped and missing teeth.

I can smell fumes and burnt rubber.

Slowly at first, then all of the sudden, everything comes rushing back to me. I am horrified, scared, and overwhelmed. What have I done?

The nightmare is always the same.

I am stuck, paralyzed, my mouth moves but no words come out, and no matter how hard I struggle I cannot speak. I cannot get anyone to hear me, to see me. I am desperately trying to get everyone's attention, to tell them it was an accident. I can hear my own voice far off in the dark distance, "...this is a mistake...I did not mean it..."

I see the memories burned in my mind, each one flashing by quickly.

A stop sign.

Blood on my hands.

A mangled wreck of two cars.

An arm sticking out of the driver's window.

The ambulance.

The hospital.

The back of the police car.

The courtroom.

The prison cell.

No matter how hard I try to speak, no sound comes out. I am pleading to be heard, to say I am sorry, to beg for it to be me instead. I can feel myself yelling, but no sounds come out. I try to make eye contact with anyone, but nobody sees me. It is as if I am not there.

Finally, the judge asks me if I have anything to say...

I turn to speak to the family.

I can finally be heard, but my words are lost among the tears. The only sounds I can make are deep, choking sobs. The chance I had is gone. I am drowning in shame, guilt, and remorse. I feel a deep self-hatred.

Those nightmares are memories, waking up provides no safe haven from the ugly truth.

My selfish and reckless choices caused the death of another young man. My inability to look around and see that my actions had consequences left a family without a son, a brother, a cousin, and a friend. No matter what I do, I cannot undo the deep pain that I have caused. Over 15 years have passed since that day and I know those wounds will never fully heal for many.

THE SINNER.

It is important that before I tell you about my greatest accomplishments in life, that I share my worst failures. This is not a story about a hero by any means, it is the story of a man who has not always done the right thing but made the conscious choice to move past those mistakes and find the ability to do some good in the world.

Most people who know me first saw me on TV, social media, or speaking at a rally about how our gym defied New Jersey's unconstitutional COVID-19 lockdowns and encouraging them to fight on their own hill – with lockdowns, masking, vaccine mandates, public school indoctrination, and many other social and political causes.

We were hailed as heroes by many, and we received the most incredible showing of love and support from hundreds of thousands – if not millions – of people all over the country and the world. We were hated too, and I was an easy target.

What is most important to know is that the courage, bravery, and grit it took to fight that battle is not a unique characteristic reserved for a select few, but something we all have. It is critically important that collectively we come to realize our strength as individuals.

My hope is that by sharing my failures and how I came to a place where I could forgive myself, heal, and find purpose in overcoming dismal circumstances, I can inspire others to do the same. We can all find our true strengths and accomplish remarkable things in life.

Perhaps if you are holding onto past mistakes that are keeping you from realizing your potential, my journey might help you let go of the past and move forward.

THE CAR ACCIDENT

The semester was ending, it was April of 2007 and finals were approaching at Stockton College. I had spent the night before doing much of the same thing that I had done for most of my college career – partying on campus while I was not at class. I did not find college particularly challenging, and I was fully embracing my juvenile and foolish pastime.

The next morning, I felt like crap. I was hungover and tired. Something told me to stay in bed, but I ignored it. I was late meeting my mom to help with some work around the house, so I got out of bed, grabbed some things to take home, and took off in my car.

For some reason that day, I did not drive my usual route home. To this day, I still do not know why I took a different path home from school. I drove well beyond the speed limit along the tree-lined backroads. This was true to my character at the time, selfish. I had no regard for anything else. I was late and that was enough justification for me to drive with such haste.

The roads were unfamiliar to me, as I entered an intersection there was a hedge on my right side, and with my excessive speed, I did not see the stop sign or the other vehicle crossing my path until it was too late to react.

Upon impact, my head smashed through the windshield. My airbag failed to deploy, and I was not wearing a seatbelt. My front teeth were knocked out, my head was cut wide open, and I was in and out of consciousness. I distinctly remember the sound of my CD player skipping.

As blood rushed down my head and covered my eyes, I was shaken from my stupor and realized the severity of what had just happened. Dazed, confused, and scared, I ran to the other vehicle to try and help. What I saw would stay with me forever. The car was horribly mangled, and it was clear that I had done something terrible. I pulled at the driver-side door with no success, I was helpless. I screamed and then blacked out.

I remember the ambulance. Looking up at the top of the vehicle. I remember the hospital. In surgery. I did not have a clear thought in my head until the doctor was examining me. My first words were "How is the other driver? Are they okay?" The doctor was cold in his response, "He's dead."

I wanted to die instead. I wanted so badly to take their place. What had I done?

My recklessness caused utter devastation for his family. Young and ignorant, I never considered that I could wake up with alcohol still present in my system from the night before. I had always viewed myself as invincible. I thought I was smarter than everyone else, that I always had it all figured out. That I was infallible. I prided myself on being someone who would drink "responsibly." I could drink and hang with the best of them if I did not get in a car that night. I had it all figured out.

In the end I was foolish, and that foolishness cost a young man his life.

By all measures this young man was a better person than me: he was a great student, loved by his community, and always willing to help others. While on the other hand, I was a troublemaker, selfish in my actions, and someone who took more than they gave.

About a week after the accident, I turned myself in to the police, being charged with Vehicular Homicide – among other things. I cried hysterically, haunted by my actions and what they caused.

I thought I knew how this interaction would go; I anticipated the same disdain that the doctor had shown me. I deserved to be hated for what I did, and I accepted that fact. Instead, I was shown compassion by the detective in charge of the case. He happened to be the first to arrive at the scene the morning of the accident. As I sat before him sobbing in shame, he said, "I know this does not make sense to you right now, but when I pulled up to the scene, I knew there were two fatalities, yet here you are. You are here for a reason. I do not know why, but that is your job to figure it out. Do not be afraid. You are going to need to find a way to forgive yourself to make sure two lives are not lost in this tragedy. Enough damage has been done. You have a responsibility to be better."

I hated myself for what I had done, and the idea of forgiveness felt foreign, unattainable, and disrespectful. Knowing that what I did could not be undone was eating me alive. No matter what I would say or do, there was no bringing him back. I could not envision my life a day ahead of where I was, let alone imagine myself being worthy of forgiveness. The detective was the first person to suggest I was worthy of forgiveness, so long as I took responsibility and earned it. I had to learn to forgive myself before I could be of use to anyone. I was at the lowest, most vulnerable point in life, and he could have easily leveled me with a few sharp words, but instead, he chose to encourage me to redeem myself by being a better man.

It would be many years before I could find the path of forgiving myself, however, this man's words stuck with me until I was ready to heal.

I never got to thank him for that, but I am sure he knew exactly what he was doing at that moment. We never really know when or how bad people are hurting, our decision to push them down or pull them up can have a much greater impact than we realize.

CHAPTER 2:

TIME TO GROW UP, KID.

"If you want to overcome the whole
world, overcome yourself."
— Fyodor Dostoyevsky

EARLY YEARS.

I did not have much of a relationship with my father. He fought his own battles during my younger years and was not much of a dad. I cannot remember one thing he taught me growing up. He eventually got his shit together, but I was in prison by the time that happened. That ship has sailed.

My mother did her absolute best to raise me. Being a single mother is about the toughest thing I think anyone could take on – even when you succeed, it is tough to fill that void in a boy's heart. She is selfless, a hard-worker, and loves more than anyone I know. Everything good about me comes from her.

We lived on our own for a while, until we moved in with her boyfriend – where we would be for more than a decade until they split. He was a very smart, successful blue-collar guy business owner. He was strict, but he taught us a lot. Every night at the dinner table he would lecture his son and I about world history, math, science, military history, and current events. He believed in having a strong work ethic too. He got pleasure out of torturing us because he knew it would harden us up. I learned a great deal from him – much of which I did not understand until later in life. For all he taught me, there was not much guidance about being a man. He battled his own demons and struggled to control his anger and temper. He worked endlessly and was consumed by his business, and like my father, they both struggled with alcohol.

After they split, we moved to an apartment a few miles away. My mom worked a lot and I had much more time on my own. I grew up shy, nervous, and scrawny. I was not the last kid picked in gym class, but I sure was not the first pick. I would easily get lost in a crowd. I was young for my grade and always felt a step behind my peers. I did not have many friends and grew up with the ones I had. I was far from my old home and friends and was forced to make new ones and began to come out of my shell. For the first time in my life, I felt seen. I was invited to new places and felt important.

By the time I was eighteen, I had racked up enough juvenile arrests and run-ins with the police to drive any parent to the brink. Always late to class and first to cut out early. On paper I made it look like I was a good student, I could squeeze out a B- with minimal effort. I was even in advanced classes. I justified my unruly behavior with my intelligence.

I grew bolder in my defiance as high school ended, so much so, that after graduating high school my mother refused to allow me to go away to college. I had to convince her I was responsible enough to go away to school. I spent my first year at community college. I earned straight A's and stayed trouble-free. The only thing I learned was that if I applied myself minimally, I was able to people to get off my back.

By the time I was in college, I was completely out of control and had no concept of what it meant to be a man. I played the tough guy role, pretended like nothing bothered me, n chased meaningless relationships with women, and prided myself on being the last man standing at a party. I walked around with an inflated ego and a dangerous sense of selfishness – a rebel without a cause.

THE REALIZATION.

After the accident, I was staying at my mom's new house at the time. It was better for me to be away from old places and circles. My friends were not bad people by any means, but I was going nowhere fast and needed to reevaluate a lot – including how I spent my free time. Weeks and months started to go by. I did not sleep much. I would stay up all night trying to avoid reliving the accident in my dreams. A handful of Tylenol PMs would sometimes give me a few hours of peace.

The years that lead up to the accident were a continuous cycle of getting in trouble, then cleaning up my mess - always setting myself back a few steps. I set the bar low for myself because I was terrified of failure, rejection, and embarrassment. If I never gave anyone anything to expect, I did not have to try and be a good man. This became a part of my identity, some sort of wannabe bad boy from suburbia. I would always fix what I did - pay the fines, do the community service, and move on. The only parent I had was my mom, and she would always forgive me. I always knew she would. She loved me. Everything she ever did was for me. I never realized how she was hurt by my mistakes because I saw them as small and insignificant. She knew the path I was heading down, and she was hurt because no matter how much she loved me, she could not save me from myself. Nobody else was affected by my mistakes so I continued to have my run-ins with the law. This time was different, however, there was no cleanup that would fix this mess.

One night, I awoke from that same nightmare.

I went to the bathroom, picking the glass out of my head. My face and head were mangled, I looked like the villain 'Two-Face' from the Batman movie. Each time I looked in a mirror, I would experience deep shame, I could not stand to look at myself for very long. That night my reflection in the mirror was slightly less difficult to look at. The reflection was the same, but the hatred I felt for myself eased slightly. The words the detective spoke to me echoed in my mind. There was nothing I could do to take away the pain I caused, but that was not an excuse for me to just check out and quit. I had a responsibility to be a better person, and by doing so, give something back to the world that I had taken so much from.

I did not go to prison until a year later, in June of 2008, which gave me time to do some meaningful things with my life before serving my time.

For the first time in my life, I had the desire to do something positive, I just did not know what that would be or how I would do it. With some encouragement from my mom, I decided to use the 14-month gap between the accident and prison to speak to high school students. By telling my story, I could warn them about the dangers that I so ignorantly chose to ignore. I was young enough for them to relate to, which gave me the ability to connect with them more than most presenters. Just a few years earlier I was one of them, now I was responsible for the death of a young man and headed to prison.

At 20 years old I had no experience in public speaking. I was a shy kid, to begin with, and at this point, I had trouble making eye contact from the deep shame I felt. I was petrified, but I knew I had to do this.

Gloucester City High School was the first school I spoke at. The auditorium was packed with three hundred students. There was a stool, a bottle of water, and a microphone on stage.

My voice shook and my legs rattled as I stood in front of that first group of students. I did not know what else I was going to say, I simply told them the ugly truth. I laid my catastrophic failures out in front of them for everyone to see. I had killed someone. I thought I would be booed off stage, but the crowd of students sat quietly and listened. The hour went quickly and there was a self of relief I experienced by publicly admitting to my mistakes. I did a private Q&A after for kids who wanted to talk to me about something personal. One young man approached and said to me, "You remind me of my older brother. He is always getting in trouble, and I am scared he could wind up like you one day. Thank you for sharing your story."

This young man's words will always stand out to me. What if I could stop others from making the same deadly mistakes that I did? I would speak at 1,000 schools if just one person learned from my story.

As we closed for the day, the school's principal shook my hand and said, "I have been doing this for 20 years, and never in my life have I seen a group of three hundred kids so quiet. You have made an impact on them. Do you mind if I give your information to some of my colleagues?"

It is because of his words that I had the confidence to speak at the next school, and the next. In the 14 months before my sentencing, I managed to speak at nearly 2 dozen schools. I never got to thank him for giving me the opportunity to clear my head and my heart, but I am sure he knew what he was doing. Just as the detective had guided me to a better life by encouraging me, this man helped me push forward too.

This made me feel alive again. It gave me a purpose and lifted some of the weight off my shoulders. It was hard to do the right thing – to tell my story – but the right thing felt good to do. Up until this point, I was barely existing. Days were spent zoning out. My cell phone would ring, and it would not even prompt me to see who was calling. I was drowning in my own sorrow. For the first time since the accident, I started to feel like there was hope for me.

Stepping off the stage that day, I got a glimpse of what it meant to be selfless, to help others, and to be a good man. I liked it and made myself a promise to be better, to be someone I was proud to be. I felt a new desire to apply myself in all the areas of my life through which I had previously applied little effort. I had been expelled from Stockton College and re-enrolled at Rutgers University. I began to take my studies seriously and impressed my professors. Grateful for second chances, I set out to make the best of it.

Waiting to get sentenced was a nerve-wracking experience, it feels like there is a countdown timer over your head - every minute passing brings you closer to the inevitable. I did my best to stay positive and productive.

With so many things out of my control, I learned to focus on the things I could change. I walked into the gym for the first time in my life after the accident and fell in love with it. My head was a mess, and my body was a wreck, but every day I left the gym I felt a little better, more accomplished, and in control. I had never built anything of significance. There had never been any long-term projects where I had to display discipline, work hard, and dedication. Working out gave me the opportunity to show myself something I had never learned before. It was a physical practice that required equal growth of my mental state. I felt more in control as I learned more about health and as my physical strength improved, my mental strength followed. I was developing my self-control and improving my confidence in a tangible way, not hiding behind a persona or some liquid courage. My appreciation for health and fitness only deepened in the years ahead.

I accomplished as much as I could between the accident and sentencing, but time had run out and I was going away. On the day of my hearing, we waited outside the courtroom. I was approached by a family member of the young man who died in the accident. I was handed a card and inside it said:

"We don't hate you; we just hate what you did."

I do not think anyone has ever said anything that has helped me more. It is one of the kindest things that I have ever experienced. This person had every right to hate me, and they chose to show forgiveness instead.

For 14 months I had worked as hard as I could to improve myself, now I had 5 years ahead of me to sit in prison, think about what I had done, and continue to become something much better than what I had to offer the world at 20 years old.

The gavel banged. The cuffs went on.

CHAPTER 3:

A prison proves the value of liberty.
— GIULIO ALBERONI

A LEARNING EXPERIENCE.

People often ask, "What was prison like?"

Well, it sucks.

It is dangerous, dirty, lonely, and cold, but most of all it is boring. It is painful watching the world go on without you as you sit on the sidelines in timeout. People quickly forget about you, and it hurts to realize how insignificant you are in the grand scheme of it all.

Although it is a harrowing experience, those same reasons can make it a place of incredible growth and transformation if you choose to take the abundance of free time and do something constructive with it. We tend to learn our best lessons through the worst pains. The space between our ears is filled with a lot that we do not understand and the scariest demons we face are always the ones within us.

Prison affords one a lot of free time, what you do with it is a choice. All I knew going in was that I did not want this to be the last chapter of my life. I was determined to make something out of this mess. I knew I did not have much control over my life, but I wanted to exercise conscious control over the elements that were within my reach.

The space between our ears is filled with a lot that we do not understand and the scariest demons we face are always the ones within us.

There were some terrible experiences and plenty of mistakes along the way, but I learned some powerful lessons that changed me for the better. I could fill a book with all the things I learned during those 5 years. There were a few moments and situations that always stand out when I look back - things that left an impression on me and led to growth.

FIRST TASTE.

The first days went by quickly, until I started to do the math. I felt an immediate and overwhelming sense of doom when I realized how far away the light at the end of the tunnel was. It felt like the walls were closing in. I knew that if I continued to think in this manner, the road ahead would be difficult. I had to stop longing for the outside world, to stop counting the days, to stop thinking about the past and the future. If I were to survive, I could only think about the day, one day at a time, and try to live my best under these new circumstances.

First, it is the county jail. The initial two weeks are rough, like camping without any gear. You get a few supplies: a toothbrush, toothpaste, an oversized shirt, oversized pants, oversized slip-on shoes, and a mattress. Jails are always overcrowded. The holding unit I was in was made for thirty-two inmates but held closer to double that. If you were lucky, you had a bed, many slept on the floors in the cells, and the unluckiest of us slept in the open dayroom – vulnerable. I spent 4 weeks there before being transferred to CRAF (Central Reception Assignment Facility) – where inmates are held until assigned to a state prison.

They come to pick you up at the jail, where you are shackled and crammed into the transport bus to be driven around the state for hours doing additional prisoner pick-ups. Upon arrival at CRAF, you are thrown into a holding cell, given a mystery meat sandwich, and a juice box. Prison life consists of a lot of waiting – your time is no longer your own. When your name is called it is off to the ice-cold showers with a sliver of soap and about thirty seconds to wash and get to the next place.

Lift your tongue.

Lift your balls.

Turn around.

Spread your cheeks.

Given a hand towel to dry off with, you get your state-issued pants, shirt, shoes, a towel, a roll of toilet paper, and a few other accessories. You are assigned your number, and this is now your name. Welcome to state prison.

The next 4 weeks were spent getting evaluated by social workers, psychologists, and other "professionals" who decide which prison to send you to. During this time, you get 60 minutes out of the cell a day to make phone calls and watch whatever garbage is on television, the rest of the time is spent sitting in a cell. I started to understand that I knew extraordinarily little about myself and that I had been running from my internal dialogue for years.

I was selected to stay in a permanent unit of CRAF, which was a privilege. The unit was small, they were the inmates who ran the kitchen and did other jobs around the facility. In comparison to most prisons, spending your time here was more like a time-out than doing hard time. Everyone on the unit was on their best behavior, so it did not seem so bad. We were not restricted to our cells all day, had some amenities that made life a little nicer, and for the most part, everyone got along.

I settled in for the first three weeks and started feeling productive. I developed a routine and was selected to work as the Chaplain's assistant. It gave me a small sense of daily purpose; this is something that is extremely challenging to maintain inside the prison walls. I enjoyed working with the chaplain, it was fulfilling to provide some help to inmates who were happy to get their hands on their holy book.

One day the chaplain asked me to help her with something on the computer and I sat down to troubleshoot for her. Less than a minute later a corrections officer [CO] walked in, saw me on the computer, threw handcuffs on me, and locked me away in solitary confinement on the third floor. That computer was connected to the internet, and this was a major infraction. I awaited a trial for a week or two in the sweltering humidity of

August. I was found not guilty because I had been instructed to sit there, but they determined the staff was too comfortable around me and shipped me off to the general population at the next facility.

Lesson learned. Sometimes bad shit just happens, even when it is not your fault you are going to have to deal with it.

WELCOME TO STATE PRISON.

My new home. There is a lot more waiting, as you are pushed through yet another intake process. Eventually, you get to where you are going to be held and you can begin to make yourself some sort of routine to productively pass the time.

This prison was a "locked down" facility, which means that unless on a job detail, the inmates are restricted to the cell for 22 hours each day with 1 hour for yard time and 1 hour in the day space to shower, use the microwave, play cards, socialize, and use the phone. The inmates at the prison were between 18 – 35. Prison is hyper-masculine, aggressive, and violent, and when you fill it with younger men it tends to be even more so. The predominant street gang in the New Jersey prison system was the Bloods, they outnumbered every other gang by large margins. This prison was their turf and they ruled it.

I would learn a lot here, quickly.

RENT IS DUE.

Everybody looks forward to their first commissary order. It is like shopping at a rundown dollar store, but in prison, which is enough to live well. If you are living off the basics that are provided, your living standard is rough. The luxury of buying an additional roll of toilet paper or bar of soap or some canned tuna to subsidize the bare minimum you are given will teach you to be grateful for the few things you have. Not everyone has people on the outside who care about them, and many come from families that struggle to make ends meet as it is, without the additional burden of sending money to prison.

On the day of the first commissary delivery, you get your order then sit around in the day room until the COs are ready to open your door. Nobody told me that it was not a good idea to order everything at once. So, there I sat in the day room with a laundry bag packed full of stuff, looking like an easy target to any hungry veteran.

Within minutes, a younger member of the Bloods approached me. He sat down and told me, "I know you are new to the unit. We are a family here. Everyone chips in $20 per order to the unit and we make sure everyone eats and everyone stays safe. Nothing bad will happen to you and if it does, we will handle it for you."

In prison this is called paying rent, essentially giving the very people who will steal your property, to protect you from getting your property stolen. Compliance with this makes for a long and uncomfortable prison sentence. Once people know you are weak and will accept anything, they will slowly continue to take more from you. Power always operates the same. It was clear to me that I could not accept that deal, no matter what. I was nervous, alone, outnumbered, and I had nowhere to go. I had been in fights before, but I never felt threatened in the way I did here. I mustered up as much courage as I could find.

Jokingly I replied, "Does this include utilities?"

He did not get the reference.

I told him that I would not be paying any rent, and he warned me that they would not help me when my property got stolen – when they stole it. I watched who he went back to give his report to, and after several minutes, approached the higher-up myself. We spoke briefly. I communicated that I was not going to be paying rent and that if my property were to go missing, I would come directly to the kid who had approached me.

He laughed and told me that I would never get a fair fight, but to do whatever I felt like I needed to.

I knew that I had to confront the inevitable and that I should do so on my own terms – not when I was unprepared or caught off guard. There was no running from this, my three choices were not great: I pay them and become subservient to the gang for the remainder of my time there, wait to get my stuff stolen and fight, or get it over with and fight now.

I had run from difficult choices my entire life, always taking the path of least resistance. I was tired of living like that. The prison was already hell; I was not going to make it any worse by being a bitch.

This was by no means my first fight, but it was by far the scariest I have encountered. Would it be broken up in time? How long would I have to fight before someone saved me from getting my head cracked? The words, "you are not going to get a fair fight" rang over and over in my head as I sat there, becoming angrier by the moment. Before I could change my mind, I tied my shoes tight and walked into the area of the day room that provided a blind spot from the guards and squared up with the guy who had initially approached me.

I entered the correctional system at six foot and a whopping one hundred and seventy pounds, comparatively this guy was easily fifty pounds heavier. None of that really mattered because I was going to get jumped by at least half a dozen of his homies anyway. My strategy was simple: hurt someone and protect myself as best I could when I was getting stomped out.

As expected, the fight went to the ground after we exchanged punches. I do not remember much – a lot of boots kicking my head and body – and a yelp from the original opponent. I had managed to get him wrapped up enough that I gave his arm elbow a good crank.

After what felt like forever, but was probably less than thirty seconds, someone yelled that the COs were coming, and they let up. As quickly as it started, it was over. The adrenaline was still pumping, I knew I would be hurting later but right then I did not feel a thing. I stood my ground and faced my fear. I felt great afterward.

Collectively, we stood around pretending like nothing had just happened. My shirt stretched and panting heavily, I tried my best to act normal. He was sitting at the phone holding his elbow, acting like he was on a call. Everyone else pretended to be occupied watching television and playing spades. The CO looked around and told us all to stand by our cells to be let in. I survived, banged up, but with my pride (and my commissary) intact.

After that day, I was never a target for extortion again.

As I would learn, it comes down to a simple risk/reward calculation for inmates. If you get caught fighting, you go to solitary confinement where you have nothing, you lose your spot on the unit, half your property will go missing and you must start all over on a new unit in 30/60/90 days. There are plenty of inmates who will bend the knee and hand over a portion of their commissary without a fight. Once it is established that you will fight – win or lose – they move onto easier, softer targets with less risk. One small sacrifice saved me 5 years of misery.

In the following weeks and months, I became friends with many of the same guys who put a boot on my head that day. It was not personal; these guys are hungry and prison life has its own set of rules. It was my rite of passage. I had earned my right to be left alone.

Lesson Learned. Face your problems head-on and stand up for yourself. Often, what you are afraid of is not as bad as you – or someone else – make it out to be.

PICK YOUR BATTLES.

Being the new guy on the unit sucks, mainly because nobody cares about you, there are not enough supplies to go around, and you do not understand the power dynamics of the group.

For the first several weeks, I did not have a pillow. Sleeping on an inch thick, ancient mattress was not comfortable, to begin with, but not having a pillow made it miserable. I complained to the guards every chance I got. My answer was the same every time, "not my problem."

I should have been figuring out a way to make a pillow until the time came when I could grab one from someone who was leaving – because that is the way it works. Instead, I complained about my situation anytime I had the chance.

I continued to pester them until I got the ear of a Lieutenant.

I was given my pillow, but it was not before one of the COs got reprimanded for it. Big mistake on my part. There is always an opposite and equal – as I would soon learn. The pillow sucked anyway – it was flat and stunk.

The guard who had gotten reprimanded also happened to be about the nastiest CO I ever came across. This guy loved his job so much that he had a tattoo on his arm of a prison key, with a snake running through it to let everyone know how much of a tough guy he was. This guy got off on making inmates' lives miserable, and it was easy for him to exact his revenge on me.

To no one's surprise, I was thrown into solitary confinement for a weapon they "found" under my flat, rancid pillow.

I was petrified at the moment, though it is funny now. I am not sure what I thought crying about how unfair life was going to achieve but it sent me right back to solitary and forced me to start over yet again.

Obviously, I had no weapon, but on the inside, you have no power to defend false statements against you made by a guard.

Sitting once again in solitary confinement, I realized I needed to wise up if I wanted to survive this experience. I was barely through the first summer of my time and I had already found myself in several bad situations.

Lesson learned. Not every battle is worth fighting. Sometimes, you just have to toughen up and endure some discomfort or take some quiet losses to save yourself the trouble of waging a war over little injustice.

UNLIKELY FRIENDS.

Upon release from solitary, you are assigned to a new unit to start all over again – that is never fun. It serves as a reminder that when you fuck up, you must work twice as hard to get back. The new cell was dirty, and it stunk. My cellmate was sleeping when I walked in. I thought to myself, "oh great" as I realized he did not have much property. I was quick to judge. When he awoke, he greeted me, and we started talking while he moved his stuff off my bunk.

What was left of my ransacked belongings had made it back to me and that was more than what he had. As I settled in, we broke bread together and started to chat over a PB&J and a cup of ramen.

"What do they call you whiteboy?"

"Ian."

"No street name?"

"Huh?"

"That's your government name, what they call you on the streets?"

"Ian."

He laughed.

"Alright Ian, they call me Weezy."

Turns out that Weezy was the highest-ranking Blood in the prison. He was an "OG" of the infamous Pirus (pronounced pie-rooz) set (a gang under the banner of a larger gang) that was originally known as the Pirus Crips, they are considered the founding members of the Bloods. An "OG" is towards the top of the food chain, only to be outranked by a double or triple OG, and a Godfather. A punk kid from the suburbs who did not know his head from his ass doing some time with a certified gangster - an odd pair for sure.

At age 30, Weezy had already spent over a decade behind bars – in and out since he was a young teen. He had 2-3 kids and had no way to support them. You could tell he was tired. Tired of life as a gang banger, being in and out of prison, and feeling like his only option was the street life.

We found common ground quickly and laughed a lot. I told him about my previous run-in with the Bloods and he assured me that it would not be happening here and that not all of them were the same – he did not believe in theft. Weezy was eager to hear about things like going to college and what suburban life was like. I was interested in learning how to not only survive in prison but how to work the system to the best of my ability – to "jail."

One of the most important things Weezy taught me was that, in prison, you must find a way to be useful. When you are useful, people do not want to mess with you because they either need or will need your help at some point. Throughout my 5 years, I found an interesting mix of services I could provide within the walls of the prison. I acted as a tutor, helping guys learn to read and prepare for the GED, I worked as a paralegal helping guys fight cases from the inside, and I found the interesting side hustle of writing love letters to the wives, girlfriends, and baby mommas of my fellow inmates. For all these services, I would accumulate friendships, favors, trades, or items in exchange for my time. The most lucrative of all was writing love letters. I would charge a handsome sum of $5 per letter, which goes a long way in the walls of the prison. The prison economy is an interesting mix of entrepreneurship and the barter system, and I learned to work it to the best of my ability.

We spent close to 20 hours a day together in the cell for the better part of a year. I helped him learn to read and study for his GED, he taught me how to handle the COs and inmates, and he always guaranteed I would at least get a fair fight. We went into business together and opened a store – which involves loaning out items for a greater repayment when the person gets their next commissary order. Though I did not have much, it was more than most guys and more than enough to start our little business. Weezy guaranteed we would not have to go chasing anyone's payment – thankfully, we never did.

We lived well together, little by little we acquired more items and were about as comfortable as you can get inside a six by nine-foot cell.

When Weezy was outside our cell he had to be different, he had to be hard – the gangbanger. It is rare that gang members leave their gang, especially after attaining high ranks. He believed his fate was sealed, but I was hopeful our time together talking about life outside of being a gang banger might somehow change things for him.

I came to know a man with a good heart, despite his sins and past actions. I was able to humanize someone the world saw as a dangerous criminal. In that, I also learned a great deal about atonement for my own actions.

One of the hardest things about prison is watching the outside world continue, while your world inside remains stagnant. We shared that experience together, it was painful, but it was something that taught me a great deal. I would never take my freedom for granted again.

The cell Weezy and I shared was not ideal, our window was stuck open, which meant it was ice-cold in the winter and hot as hell in the summer. In the winter we had to sleep with as many layers of clothing as possible, we would each plug-in our hot pots (an electric kettle) and lay in our bunks with them through the frigid nights. In the summer we made tents out of bunks, with a tiny fan fashioned by our feet, blowing air on us. We were grateful for the comfort we did have and creative enough to mitigate the miserable parts of prison. It is easy to be negative inside the walls, but that mindset will slowly eat you alive. We still managed to laugh and make the best of it – even through the worst of it.

I checked on him many years later and he had returned to prison on new charges. At the time of writing this, he has been out for over 5 years. I hope he is living a good life, wherever he is. To this day, I still think about him. I learned so much during the time we spent living in those confines. Two different men, from two hugely different worlds. We became close friends despite our differences, and I know he made me a better man, I can only hope I had the same impact on him.

Lesson learned. Be open-minded and slow to jump to judgment. You can learn something from everyone, and you should.

NOT EVERYONE WHO IS
FRIENDLY IS YOUR FRIEND.

The first year and a half went by quickly – as quickly as it can in prison. Once you settle into a routine, get your commissary orders going, some books, make some friends, a job (if you are lucky), and some visits on the weekends, the days start to pass into weeks and the weeks into months and the months into years.

Life was about as good as it could be. The COs knew me and understood I was not going to cause any trouble; they tend to be less restrictive on you when they figure that out. I settled into a position as a GED tutor and law clerk, so a lot of the higher-ranking gang members who were looking to parole early or were fighting other charges owed me favors for helping them. I got rather good at spades, hearts, poker, and dominos. We laughed a lot. In prison, you are either mad, sad, or funny. People develop a healthy sense of humor to deal with pain. It was not home, but it was not hell either.

The GED classroom I worked in had a few other tutors in it. They were decent dudes, many of them Aryan Brotherhood [AB]. AB had always tried to get me to join, along with every other gang. I got good at saying no and made it a point to be friendly with most people.

One day, an AB inmate asked me to pass a message along to one of his friends who lived on my unit. No problem. No big deal. He asked again a week or so later. Sure, no problem. One more time a few weeks later. Yeah, I got you bro.

This time was different, he handed me a note, all taped up. It looked like a note you would have passed in school before we all had cell phones. I was not happy about it, but we were already in the hallway moving back toward our units. We were not allowed to have anything in our pockets, and definitely not a note from one gang member to another. I stuffed it in my sock and moved quickly.

In most prisons, they have "movements" or predetermined times throughout the day when the inmates who are working, at school, the yard, or somewhere else in the prison head back to their cells. The COs line the hallways and look for anything suspicious, prevent inmates from killing each other, and pull over random inmates for searches.

It was my lucky day.

"Smith! Get over here," a familiar CO said.

Hopefully, it is a quick one, I thought as I stood facing the wall with my hands up.

"Shoes off," he said.

He finds the note and proceeds to read it as I get slammed up against the wall by two more COs. I could taste the lead as my head got pushed into the crusty, old wall. The note was drug-related, a big shipment coming in. I do not know what else was in there, but it was not good. Away I went to the hole again.

This was my longest stay in solitary – a couple of weeks. I was so angry – at the AB inmate, at the CO, at everyone except myself. I was comfortable where I was on my unit and now that was all gone – again.

Solitary confinement is a weird place. You are in a tiny cell by yourself, with nothing. There is little to no noise on the unit, as most of those cells are built like bomb shelters. No windows. You have a bed and a sink/toilet combo. You do not ever come out, except to take a shower every few days – if you are lucky. You get surprisingly good at washing your ass in the sink to combat the stench of your own odor. There is a lot that sucks about it. The worst part is the silence – it is deafening. You have 24 hours a day to sit and think – you can only sleep for so many hours. All there is to do is sit and think about your life – the things you miss, the wrongs you have done, the fears you have, and all the thoughts you can normally drown out with a TV show, a night out, or whatever you use to escape. There is no running from what is in your head. It is terrifying to face yourself, but if you do, it is one of the most empowering experiences you will ever live through.

I am thankful for that time. This is also where I first gained my appreciation for exercise – something that would later become a passion and develop into a lifestyle and a career. No matter what was going on in my little world, I had something to tether onto. I could always get down on the ground and do some pushups. I could always move. I could always get my heart rate jacked up. I could always release the stress in a positive manner. Every fear I had, every doubt, every regret, and every ounce of pain became manageable as I sat with my thoughts and worked out until my heart pounded out of my chest – reminding me I was alive. When it was over, I had gone through a long series of realizations about myself that I may have never pushed through had I not been stuck in that cell.

When you know what you are afraid of, what you have been running from, and why you act the way you do, you become incredibly empowered as an individual. You are no longer a victim of your emotions – conscious or unconscious. I also learned to accept personal responsibility for even the things that I would have previously said: "were not my fault." Although he had not warned me at all about the contents of the note, there was nobody to blame but myself for putting myself in the position to get screwed like that.

The Classification Board decided that I was to be moved to a new prison – one too many strikes. And off I went.

Lesson learned. Internal dialogue is an important part of growth. We tend to mute it with distractions in our lives. Learning to listen to myself and not run from it brought me a level of personal accountability that I lacked.

ONE AND DONE.

The new prison had many of the same characters, with a different ratio of inmates. This new dynamic changes the rules, as the balance of power is different. In this prison, the Bloods were still the most populous gang, but the Crips, Latin Kings, Ñeta, and Whiteboys had a much stronger presence here.

Most of the units here were dormitory style, with sixty-six men to a unit sleeping on thirty-three bunks. The dorm was loud, chaotic, smelly, and often dangerous. It is hard to let your guard down when there are that many people around you. The bathroom is a shitty experience – pun intended. It is all open and the sinks are right next to the toilets, and the toilets face each other in rows with walls between them. Brushing your teeth to the stench of a grown man passing prison slop is not ideal, and neither is sitting across from another man while you take a dump. You get used to it though.

I settled in, made friends, and got into my daily routine and time started to pass.

It was in this prison where I witnessed some of the worst violence I have ever seen. Because the ratio of gangs was more balanced, there was more jockeying for power. The open style of living led to the inevitability of men clashing. Fights were much more common, and in many units, it was a daily occurrence. Everybody fought at some point, and most of it was harmless – the settling of disputes, guys butting heads, and jockeying for hierarchy. There were times it was not so harmless too. Watching a grown man scream after a bowl of boiling hot water, mixed with melted Vaseline, and packets of spice from Ramen noodles was thrown in his face was about the most disturbing thing I had ever witnessed, until it was not.

Gangs self-govern in interesting ways, usually, it involves violence. Violence is a part of gang life, and it is how they keep each other in line within the organization. There are varying levels of discipline any out-of-line member will receive, depending on the gang. It was common to see guys go into the back of the dorm with a few of their homies and put their hands up while they get jumped. They are not allowed to fight back for 30 seconds or whatever was commanded. The Crips had a particularly brutal one, it was called "hardcore." The hardcore is reserved for the most serious infractions. In this case, the inmate on the receiving end of the hardcore represented a Crip set that had been disgraced and thus disbanded. He was a baby, barely eighteen. They gave him the choice to join a recognized set or a hardcore. He chose to stand with his gang and refused.

The only rule of a hardcore is that a hardcore has no rules. There is no set time, no restriction to where or how you can be attacked, no limit on the people involved, and no ability to ask for mercy.

In the back of the 66-man dorm, we heard them beat this boy within inches of his life, a dozen of them, savagely stomping on his skull until he lay lifeless on the cold, hard cement. By the time the COs had figured out what was happening, called for backup, and arrived, it was too late to save him. He died shortly after at the hospital.

Eating dinner later that day, I looked around to see the same guys who took part in it laughing and telling jokes, the brutality had no effect on them. I sat and thought. The young man's death brought up feelings of guilt and shame about the life I had taken. I had been shaken out of my routine. So many days go by in prison where it's the same boring thing – breakfast, shower, play some cards, go to the yard, read a book, call your family, watch some TV – that you can forget that many of the people you are living with have zero respect for life – even their own. I never wanted to come back to this place.

There were many dark moments like this, but I learned so much from them. It most definitely forced me to grow up, harden up, and man up. To survive I developed courage, confidence, competence, and people skills. Even in the worst of times, prison made me grow stronger – inside and out.

BEST OF FRIENDS, THE WORST OF TIMES.

I met one of my best friends, Evan, in prison. It has been a decade since we have both been released, and he is more like a brother than a friend.

Evan and I both had good jobs in the prison, and special privileges because of it. We lived on separate units but met each other one morning in the yard for a special yard time dedicated to certain inmates with higher work status.

We walked laps around the big yard in the chilly morning, kicking a soccer ball back and forth while talking about where we were from, life on the outside, and everything else. By the end of yard time that morning we were inseparable. When we were together it did not feel like a prison, it just felt like hanging out with your friend. We traded stories about girls, shared our goals and dreams for what we wanted to do when we both got released, kept each other's spirits high, and motivated one another to continuously focus our time on getting better.

As we both achieved minimum security status around the same time, we were assigned to the "camps" – a unit with very few COs or security. If you are in the camps, you are on the back end of your sentence, where life gets better and there are fewer restrictions and more allowances.

Our work detail was called Greystone and the job was to tend the grounds of Greystone Psychiatric Hospital in Morris County, NJ. The hospital was located on a huge, steep hill and the grounds were massive. Out of ten guys assigned to the detail, only six went out every day – first come first serve. Work was a treat for us, we were grateful for every moment outside of the prison walls, no matter how backbreaking the labor was. We would mow acres of grass in the scorching summer heat and shovel snow in the coldest winters with smiles on our faces – anything to feel free.

Every morning we would wake up at 4:30 am to workout, eat, shower, and sprint to be the first in line to work. Evan and I taught each other gratitude. Those last two years were not so bad, because we learned to make the best of the worst. We learned to find the one thing to be happy about, even though there was plenty to be upset about.

The officer assigned to this detail was a decent guy, he saw how hard we worked and would allow us a tiny bit of latitude to have some fun.

He would let us bang music loudly in the van, with the windows down, staring at the beautiful women in sundresses as we drove through town. He had let us mess around on our breaks: go explore the woods, race each other up the huge hills and wrestle our way down, let us wander through the abandoned old building, play pranks on each other, along with a million other things that made us feel free.

Being in nature brought us a sense of peace and freedom that I will always remember. We were like wild dogs being let out of their cages every day. We lived for these moments. There was a stream off in the woods that became our lunch spot; we would hunt for wild berries and sit with our legs in the stream and eat lunch – happy with what little we had and hopeful for our future.

To this day, many of the habits I formed during this time still stick with me – rise early, workout daily, find joy in little things, spend time outside, and always look for the silver lining. Prison taught me to appreciate what most overlook– good friendships, laughter, and the pride that comes with a job well done.

Our friendship is just as strong today as it was when we were two twenty-something-year-olds with nothing but dreams in our heads. The lives we fantasized about living have become reality, better than we could have ever imagined. I was proud to stand next to Evan at his wedding last month. If you gave me the choice of not having to serve any time but never meeting Evan, I would gladly do the time again.

ALMOST HOME.

As the time runs down on the clock, the back end is not so bad. Eventually, if you are good, you get released to a halfway house, where you can get a job, go to school, and start to assimilate back to life as a normal person. Evan and I wound up going to separate locations.

In the halfway house, you go through the intake process all over again. At first, you are not permitted to leave, but once you go through the process, you get a taste of freedom. You are not allowed to have a car and many other things like cash and a cell phone, but you can get yourself a job. I had planned ahead based on some tips I received from other inmates who had been through the process before and with a job already lined up and my college application submitted, I went right to a decent routine. The feeling of being allowed back into society after you have been exiled and had every freedom stripped from you is a powerful experience. I had previously hated college but was now happy to be a student again. I got a job as a personal trainer and set out to pursue my dream of sharing my passion with the world. Fitness saved my life and transformed me into a new person. I wanted to share that with the world.

We broke all the rules in the halfway house as soon as we could. They let you go home on the weekends – for eight hours, then sixteen, then thirty-two, and forty-eight – if you do not mess it up.

Evan and I were done waiting to live our lives, so we would forward our house lines to our cell phones to throw off the social workers who staffed the houses. We were inseparable and insatiable – we wanted to see and do everything, go everywhere, talk to everyone, and experience everything we had missed for 5 years. We damn sure did. I can remember countless times we would be out at an ungodly hour of the morning and one of our cell phones would ring, you would see us bolt for the door only to return a few minutes later with a smile on our faces – right back to living our lives.

WE WERE ALMOST HOME...

Of all the lessons learned in those 5 years, having gratitude is by far the most powerful, useful, and important of them all. Prison built me. It took me losing everything to understand that I had all I needed. It forced me to explore the things that hurt me - my mistakes, fears, excuses, and sins. To survive and not be swallowed by the experience, I had to learn to be happy with nothing - happy with myself. When you can find happiness where others cannot, find joy even when suffering, and celebrate the things that most take for granted, you become hard to stop.

CHAPTER 4:

FREEMAN

Everything negative - pressure, challenges -
is all an opportunity for me to rise.
- Kobe Bryant

A QUIET RIDE HOME.

Ready to go home. Get that final prison haircut, that final shave. Give all your stuff away to the guys still doing time. Say your goodbyes and see-you-laters. Play those last few hands of spades. Talk some shit with the guys you are leaving behind one last time. Sleep on that crappy-old mattress, on that rusty old bunk bed one last time.

It was a quiet, cool, gray morning. As I walked out into the parking lot, deep gratitude and euphoria came over me. There was no big celebration, no cheers for joy, or crowds of people, it was just a regular day. I had yearned for a regular day for 5 years and it was finally here. The car ride was quiet and peaceful. There was not much that needed to be said, but there was much to think about, appreciate, and reflect on.

It was finally over.

Every fear I had was gone, I had made it to the other side. I thought about the lost boy who walked in and was proud of the young man who walked out. For as far as I had come, I knew there was a long road ahead of me. I had promised myself and many others that I would be a better man, and be a force for good in my family, my community, and in the world around me. Serving my time was just the first step in fulfilling those promises.

The world looked different than it had before – it was full of possibilities, potential, challenges, and conquests. With a new work ethic, a deep appreciation for life, a mission to give back, and a voracious appetite for personal growth I was ready to hit the ground running.

I thought about the card I had been handed on the day of my sentencing and how much I owed to the people I had hurt, to my family and loved ones for supporting me, and to the world for the damage I had caused.

I did not have a big plan, but I knew a few things. Working out had been something that radically changed my life for the better – confidence, discipline, mental toughness, a positive self-image, and constructive self-talk. Exercise saved my life, and I knew that I could make people's lives better by sharing what I had learned by working out and committing to being healthy.

BEHIND THE 8-BALL.

On top of all the pain and suffering the automobile accident brought about, there was significant financial damage that had put me into deep debt – even without that, starting fresh at 26 years old is not a place most people want to be.

In the halfway house I had been working as a personal trainer at a small local gym, it was a start, but not what I had envisioned for how I wanted to make my mark on the world. In the meantime, I took some additional jobs to help myself catch up financially. School was going well; I spoke several more times about my car accident and time in prison and wrote frequently about it in my school newspaper and other publications.

When you find yourself behind your peers, it can be incredibly motivating. I looked around at the people I knew growing up and saw people buying homes, graduating college and graduate school, having children, and excelling in their careers.

I longed for those things. As happy and grateful as I was to be free, it ate away at me that I was a grown man living at home with my parents. The choices were simple: work harder or continue to feel inadequate. Nobody was going to save me or do it for me, so I kicked it into overdrive.

BREAKING OLD CYCLES.

Over the next few years, I climbed out of debt, moved across the country, graduated from Arizona State University, saved up some money, and proceeded to make a series of poor choices that left me broke, back living with my parents, and licking my wounds.

I had been hired as the Assistant General Manager of 24-Hour Fitness and was performing better than anyone had anticipated. I was proud of my accomplishments in the fitness industry in such a short amount of time. Two weeks into that job, a man in a suit walked into my office and told me to pack my stuff – that HR had decided they did not want to employ me because of my prior felony convictions. Soon after that, I moved home. The wind had been knocked out of my sails.

Life was starting to feel like it had before I went away – an endless cycle of me doing well, only to make bad choices and set myself back. I could feel myself falling into the victim mentality that so many suffer from. No matter how hard I tried to work, my past followed me like a dark cloud. Deep down I did not feel worthy of living a good life. "Who was I to be happy?" I would ask myself. I began to get discouraged and started to engage in destructive habits again – I spent my time chasing women, gambling, and hanging with people who were going nowhere. I blamed others for my shortcomings. It was not my fault I was not making a lot of money; it was because people were biased against me for being an ex-felon. I did not believe my own lies, but it did not stop me from trying to fool myself.

If you look hard enough, there is always someone to blame. You can always find an external reason you are not doing what you need to be doing to live the life you want. That is the easy way out and most people take it at some point, and many will live their entire lives like this. It is easy in the short-term to adopt this behavior, it saves you from the uncomfortable reality that you are to blame for where you are. In the long term, it is one of the most destructive thing people do to themselves. Your fault or not, the world does not care what is holding you back from accomplishing your goals.

Eventually, I hit bottom. It was not one thing, it was everything. I was walking around with a mask on, just as I had done in the years before my accident. I was miserable, pretending to be happy. Distracting myself with things that lead me nowhere, that only took from me, and that did not get me closer to my goals. I certainly was not adding any real value to the world around me, like I had promised myself I would do. I thought about the 26-year-old man who learned to be happy in a prison cell, the young man who always found the good in any situation. That man would have been disgusted that I lost the spark, my sense of gratitude, and abandoned my promise to be the best version of myself. I thought about how much had been lost because of my actions. I thought about how much my mother had sacrificed to help me through it all. I had only been out of prison for a few years, and I was slipping.

I felt a familiar, deep sense of shame.

I was mediocre at best.

This is what I would do with my second chance?

Hitting my stride.

After being fired from 24 Hour Fitness, I promised myself that I would never work for anyone again. Truth is, I was never a great employee, even when I was a good one. This was one of the most powerful experiences of my life; it hurt badly, but it forced me into the idea of small business and entrepreneurship – something for which I am thankful.

Back in New Jersey, I had no clients and no idea where to start. I realized social media would be a powerful tool to get my name out as a personal trainer. I put out some basic information about my services and that I was taking on clients. I needed to work so badly that I made it clear I would travel and train in any accommodations. On my already maxed-out credit cards, I bought dumbbells, a sledgehammer, found myself some ropes, an old tire, and a few other tools I could use to train people.

I leveraged social media to display the accomplishments of the people I was working with, and it grew quickly. It was a simple and effective model. When I started working out, I remembered the feelings of pride and change in my confidence when I would be able to accomplish a new task or get better at others. By filming short videos of my clients achieving something they had previously assumed they could not do and posting it online, they were quick to share the video because they were happy and wanted to show their friends and family their personal growth. Each time a client shared something, my business was exposed to a new network of people, and it was free. One client turned to two, two turned to four, four turned to eight, and before I knew it, I was working twelve hours a day, traveling all over NJ and PA. This eventually led to a personal training business averaging ninety one-hour sessions per week. During my first week of training, I only had two sessions, and less than a year later I had too many clients to continue traveling. I had proven to myself that the only thing that ever held me back from being great was my own stupidity and excuses. There was no magic to it - just hard work and dedication.

Being a small business owner began to shape me in positive ways. Being in business is tough, even on the good days. Just as prison had forced me to adapt and grow, running my own little personal training operation put me through challenges that required personal development. I worked, lived, and improved my craft. My life improved in immeasurable ways after I made the decision to work for myself. There is a certain freedom in self-employment that is priceless - many learned this during the forced vaccinations of 2021-2022. That freedom is earned through the personal development and effort required to run a business successfully.

I remember being told by many that I should consider a real job, and that I would never make any real money being a personal trainer. My whole life I would be quick to accept an excuse not to do something, be it my own or someone else's. One thing you will hear a lot in business is that the market is saturated. Truth is, no matter what market you are in, you will face competition. Most people in any industry will be doing the minimum to get by. Differentiating yourself with a unique approach and putting the customer relationship above the transaction is the cheat code to success. I did not build to ninety sessions a week until I had the foundation of nine regular sessions a week. Too many times people focus on the big dream rather than properly executing the small steps it takes to get there. One session at a time. This was the first time in my life I thought like this, and it paid off tremendously.

Eventually, I rented space in the back of a local nutrition store. The owner would later become my business partner at the gym. He gave me a great deal and allowed me the freedom to build whatever I wanted in the unused space. I slowly began to create my make-shift personal training studio by reinvesting every dollar I made back into the business. My days would start before sunrise and run until long after dark. The new space allowed me to serve more clientele with better equipment and improved the value of my training. For the first time in years, I was proud of myself. It was incredible to witness the changes in clients' lives and rewarding to know that I was able to positively impact my community by teaching exercise and health.

In one year, I went from training people in the park out of the trunk of my car to having my first own personal training studio. I had built something meaningful and positive. It was nice being an asset to the community, rather than a liability. This continued to grow throughout the next year. I developed a name for myself in the local area as one of the most sought-after trainers and began to develop an online following from the work I had put in.

Building a business will not happen overnight, it requires hard work, sacrifice, and discipline. Success requires sacrifice – as I learned. The social life I once held in high regard was put on the back burner, my spending habits changed, and overall, my priorities shifted. I was growing.

The relationship between my business and the nutrition store grew alongside each other, my clientele spilled over into the store and vice versa. My own skillset evolved as I became more knowledgeable about supplements and nutrition. As I began to max out on the ability to take new clients, I began to look elsewhere for new ways to bring in revenue. The business I had built was rewarding but was one-dimensional in nature. If I worked, I would make money, but if I took a day off, I would make no money. I was tied so closely to the success of my business that I could not step away from it. I found myself handcuffed to my operation. Business would force me to learn and grow. I took my services online and coached people around the country, started an apparel line, and began to slowly scale my small operation.

CAUGHT UP.

With all these positive strides I had been making, there were still some serious things that I needed to work on. After my first two years of training, I had no money in my bank account to show my success.

Why? I had been busy celebrating my small success every weekend with expensive dinners, material possessions, and vacations. The frugality I had learned and practiced for so many years went right out the window. I worked like a savage for years with little to show for it.

How foolish. The first taste of success went straight to my head. Everything I made was spent celebrating and trying to keep up with peers who were in business for multiple years. I was so desperate to appear successful that I was hindering my own ability to grow.

I took a good hard look at myself and kept it real. Would I fall into the same cycle of self-destruction or fix the behavior? This was a familiar fork in the road for me, and typically I would cover for my own behavior. It would have been easy to remind myself that I was a successful small business owner and that I was making a nice income. But the truth was, this was not my best, and that is what I had promised. I set guidelines on how I was going to live my life, cut out unhealthy habits, created a budget to save, and began planning a future for myself outside of the day-to-day routine.

It took me 32 years to figure it out, but the picture was starting to come in clearly. Despite the many missteps along the way, I was proud of what I had accomplished. In a matter of a few years, I had radically improved myself, paid off my debt, built a business that helped people, and most importantly, grown as a man.

CHAPTER 5:

THE AMERICAN DREAM

"Entrepreneurship is the last refuge
of the trouble-making individual."
- Natalie Clifford Barney

DO YOU WANT TO BUY A GYM?

The offer came one day while I was training, the nutrition store owner walked into my area of the shop and asked if I wanted to partner with him on a second location. It would be inside a local gym about 20 minutes away. This was an incredible opportunity he was presenting, and I jumped on it.

The new location was set up quickly, but soon realized that the foot traffic in the gym was less than we had thought. The gym was in an excellent location and had tons of great equipment and potential but the owner at the time was split between this facility and the others that he operated. Gyms are a dime a dozen, so without the presence and influence of the owner, good management, and staff they lack a lively environment and blend in with the competition.

A few weeks later, my business partner burst into the room and asked me, "Do you want to buy the gym with me?"

Immediately I responded with a yes, though I had no idea where I was going to produce the money to do so. I just put all my funds into the nutrition store we opened less than a month earlier. Thanks to some great friends and family who had faith in my ability to make this venture work, I was able to secure enough to purchase the struggling gym.

With haste, a deal was brokered for us to take over. 60 days after opening our nutrition store, we became the new owners of a failing gym in Bellmawr, New Jersey. No lawyers were involved, no checking of the equipment to make sure it was all fully functional, no formal partnership agreement, and no inspection of the facility other than some walkthroughs. We should have taken the time to do our due diligence, but our minds were set on buying it and nothing was going to change that. With plenty to do, we went straight to work.

A DUMPSTER FIRE.

To be honest, I would have bought the gym even if it had no members and all the equipment was broken. It did not matter to me. What I saw in it was the potential to create a top-tier facility that – at the time – south Jersey lacked. A place where people came to grow strong – physically and mentally – and push past the limits they had previously set on themselves.

It turned out that the facility needed a lot of love and some critical issues had been left out by the previous owner as we brokered the deal. I learned to see it for what it was. It was my choice to buy in a hurry, I would not be mad at the salesman if I walked onto a used car lot and bought the car on the spot without driving it or having a mechanic look it over properly, so I had nobody to be upset with but myself.

Having to work on the plumbing, HVAC, and electrical slowed us down, but it never held us back. We hit the ground running to revitalize the quiet, dying facility. We worked tirelessly as we repaired the broken equipment, reorganized the layout, built a new culture, and brought our vision to life.

It took twelve and fourteen-hour days, seven days a week and all our energy, but in the first month we had paid the bills and put money back into the business. This was demanding work, but it was easy to do, because we just created a place where we would want to work out. We knew exactly what needed to be done and we did it. It was simple – work hard, invest back into the business, and create an environment where people feel respected, appreciated, and encouraged.

In three months, we held a huge grand re-opening party that was attended by a thousand people from all over New Jersey and the surrounding states. Our gym was an epic success. I was on top of the world. Just a few short years earlier, I moved home at thirty years old with nothing but credit card debt, a badly bruised ego, and no direction. Now, I was standing among a thousand people who had come from all over to celebrate the success that the gym had become seemingly overnight. From training people in parking lots to owning a facility where hundreds of people came every day to get healthier, stronger, and better. The young man of my past could have never imagined he would be capable of something like this.

After the big party, we resumed work on improving the equipment and building the membership base. We worked tirelessly, but it was invigorating to be building our business together. Every day at work our members became more like family, our reach grew, and there was always great energy in our facility. We breezed through the holidays, enjoying being open on Christmas Day and New Year's Day. Our members were so die-hard that we would have a packed house every day, even on those holidays when everyone else took the day off. We pledged to be open 365 days a year – a promise we would keep.

BUILDING A FAMILY.

As new gym owners, we opened our space in the gym to local personal trainers, coaches, and therapists. We wanted to foster that same symbiotic relationship that I had as a trainer in the old nutrition store. We were happy to help other small businesses grow alongside ours.

We only had one office, but we would rearrange it several times a week to transform it into a makeshift massage therapy room. It gave me pleasure to see all these people do remarkable things inside our facility – we were able to provide a place for them to do what they love, and they repaid us by helping the gym grow.

This setup became increasingly challenging once the spotlight was on us during the COVID fight. There were phone calls with our lawyers, phone and TV interviews - many were done inside the supply closet or inside my truck.

We had an upward trajectory; the hard work was paying off wonderfully. We exceeded every goal we set, and it was undeniable that we were one of the best facilities in our corner of the world. Life was simple and good. We hosted events regularly and the culture of the gym was thriving.

Then we began hearing chatter about a killer virus in China that originated in a wet market from some guy eating bat soup. People started acting strange, panic buying toilet paper. Until then, I did not pay much attention to events outside of work at the gym. Something felt off, none of this seemed real.

CHAPTER 6:

FOURTEEN DAYS TO SLOW THE SPREAD

"Decision is a risk rooted in
the courage of being free."
— **Paul Tillich**

9 MONTHS.

Everyone knows this part of the story.

We heard the news of a novel virus. America turned to the media for information. They showed us videos of people dropping dead in the streets of China. It started with mentions during the normal broadcasts, then the panic spread, and the death count was put up in the corner of every newscast. Twenty-four hours a day it was covered. COVID-19 was the big one and it was coming for all of us.

What started as whispers and speculation about a national shutdown, grew into public discussion, and eventually the order to close all non-essential businesses came in March of 2020 – just 9 months after we bought the gym. After all the money, time, and effort we had put into making it a success, shutting down was the last thing we wanted to do. This was an absolute nightmare.

I can clearly remember the days leading up to the shutdown order. We were skeptical about whether it would happen, but even the idea of allowing the government to shut us down did not sit well with many in the gym – members and owners alike. That last day in the gym was surreal. We had built an incredible environment in just nine months, and now we were being told we had to close. We were terrified by the idea, but unfortunately, we did not understand the situation confidently enough to remain open.

There was plenty of work to do at the gym, so we kept busy in the first days of the shutdown. It was eerie driving down the empty highway, pulling into the silent parking lot at the strip mall where the gym is located, and walking into a quiet, cold facility. Day one of the shutdown was our first of many red flags. As I was working out towards the end of the day, a member and Bellmawr police officer walked in and told us that someone had taken a picture of me, working out alone in our fourteen-thousand square foot gym and sent it to the county Health Department. They called the police and instructed them to advise us that if I did not stop working out, we would be given a $50,000 fine and lose our business license. When we asked for some documentation, there was none to produce.

The whole thing stunk already.

Within a few days of the shutdown, we heard about other businesses struggling, people talking about how they could not make it much longer, and some businesses beginning to shut down. We invested everything into making our dreams a reality and the thought of not surviving the shutdown was terrifying.

WHO, WHAT, AND WHY?

Having been shut down, we wanted to understand who the people were who had made the decision to shut us down and what we were all so afraid of. We began to follow what was happening in politics and set out to study the science of

COVID. After the initial fear had worn off, it became clear that the media was not informing Americans – it was scaring them. We went to work doing our own research, with a hunch that we were not being told the truth. Even worse, it was also clear that our politicians were playing politics as usual.

The more we learned about the "official" science and politics of the shutdown, the less sense it made. Our suspicions were confirmed, when on day eleven of the shutdown Congress passed the single biggest spending bill in American history – a whopping $2.2 trillion. In that bill – which most people have never read – was all the convincing we needed to reopen our business. It was clear we were not going to open anytime soon. With 3 days left of the original two weeks that they asked businesses to close, they started giving people money to stay home, offered financial incentives for states to unnecessarily test, and much more.

It was obvious they were not going to lift the mandates. Facing the ugly truth that politicians were going to destroy our business, we decided we were going to reopen. There were more questions than answers and a lot of work to be done. Once again, we resumed our long days back at the gym, beginning our preparations for who knew what.

What was happening was wrong – there was no denying that. I watched countless small businesses in the local area crumble under the weight of the restrictions – gyms, restaurants, hair salons, daycares, and more. People I knew owned these businesses, good people, who work hard and add value to their communities. Many of those that shut their doors forever were multi-generational businesses that had been built through great sacrifice and provided a good life for middle-class American families. This bothered me. All of this went on as we watched the rich get richer. There was no shutdown for the big box stores and profits soared while Middle America burned.

There were many of us around the country who felt this way – the early adopters, the initial resistance. We communicated online and spoke about our grievances, and we were demonized for having such thoughts by what felt like most people. As we began our preparations at the gym, we set out to create a robust safety protocol that went above and beyond what anyone else that was open was required to do. If corporations like Walmart could be safe, so could every small business, church, and school in America. We intended to prove this to the world – no matter what the cost.

It was decided that we were going to give them 2 months from the day of closure. They had asked for "2 weeks to slow the spread" and in that time they made it clear that there was no real plan to reopen. In fact, the plan had changed, and the American people were now subject to ongoing mandates and restrictions until they were told they could resume a normal life. It was all in the name of "health." They were keeping us safe, they said. Except it did not feel like that at all.

We had 6 weeks to prepare, educate ourselves, and formulate a game plan for what was ahead. We knew it was not likely that the government was to cooperate, and we also knew that there was a good chance they would attack us for opening our businesses. Stories began to pop up in the news about businesses that were trying to open. As we approached our reopening, I saw the news coverage of a man named Louis Uridel being led out of his California gym in handcuffs and a woman named Shelley Luther ripping up citations outside of her Texas hair salon with armed citizens protecting her business from closure. I became great friends with both through the fight ahead. I can clearly remember the feelings of excitement, anxiety, fear, and hope that came from watching these two brave Americans be the first to breach the big lie. Our gym would be next, and there would be no compromise with the tyranny of Governor Phillip Murphy.

Time was winding down and we finalized the details of our reopening, our safety protocol was ready, and it was time to announce to the world our plan for not only our small business to reopen, but the plan for any small business, church, and school in the country to reopen safely.

GAS ON THE FIRE.

About a week before we reopened, we advised local police and government of our plan to reopen. We did so as a courtesy, it was not our intent to cause trouble or be reckless, we were opening because we had to and because it was the right thing. I sat down in front of my phone and filmed a 9-minute video explaining who we were, what we planned to do, why we were doing it, and how we were going to keep our members and the community safe. I rewrote the words dozens of times, and the video took at least forty attempts. Finally, I got it done. I took a deep breath and hit send. This was getting real.

I watched as the view count went up – first by the hundreds and then the thousands – then the comments started to pour in with equal parts praise and criticism. Immediately, we became heroes to some and villains to others, but we knew in our hearts what we were about to do was the right thing. We were comfortable with being criticized, no matter how uncomfortable it would be because we were not willing to accept the lies that we were being told.

Rarely is the right choice also the easy one to make. This would not be easy, but I had no doubts we were doing the right thing. I remembered some of the challenging choices I had to make in prison, and how it had always worked out.

That night a friend of mine recommended that I send my video to a Philadelphia radio host, Rich Zeoli. He said Rich would be interested in covering the story. I did and received an almost immediate response. We were to go on the show the next morning and talk about our plans. We did. He had us on for fifteen minutes and the conversation had my palms sweaty and my mouth dry. This was getting even more real.

Another friend and client of mine suggested to me that I should go for more media, that we were going to need exposure if we were going to be able to stay open. She suggested 'The Tucker Carlson Show' and I laughed, thinking it was impossible. By the end of the day, she had tracked down one of the executive producers of the show and told him about what was set to happen.

My phone rang while I was training with a client.

"Hello?"

"Hello. Is this Ian Smith?"

"Yes."

"This is a producer from the Tucker Carlson Show. Are you reopening your gym against lockdown orders?"

"Yes, we are."

"Do you want to come on the show and talk about it?"

"When?"

"Tonight. We need you at the studio in 4 hours."

Stunned, "Yes. Absolutely."

My heart was already racing. We had hoped for one source of local media to pick up the story, so we did not get crushed by the government without people knowing. Even before we reopened, the most-watched cable news show in history would feature our story during the opening monologue.

I went on Tucker Carlson that evening, exactly one week before we would throw our doors open. At a small satellite studio in Philadelphia, I sat in a dark room in front of a backdrop of the skyline, hooked up to mics, staring at a camera, hearing the show in my ears, and watching myself on the TV screen.

The show started, Tucker began his opening monologue and my heart started pounding in my chest. I looked down at my chest and could physically see my shirt flutter with each thunderous beat. Tucker said "...a New Jersey Gym..." and my heartbeat grew so loud I could feel and hear it in my ears. I could barely hear his voice as he introduced me, the entire world faded, and I kicked into autopilot.

I remember little of that first conversation with Tucker, except when he asked, "you are on the most watched news show in the country, and you are about to openly defy your Governor's orders to close your business. Are you ready to do that?"

I answered calmly, "Yes."

And if it was not real before, it was now.

When I realized the interview was over. I looked at my phone, it was buzzing so furiously with notifications it was sliding off the table. I picked it up and saw dozens of missed calls and voicemails from family and friends, easily a hundred text messages and notifications popped up on my screen. They were coming in so fast I could not keep up. The response was overwhelmingly positive, any hatred was drowned out. People were ready for this fight and celebrated us just for talking about reopening.

THE DOORS WILL OPEN MONDAY.

Governor Phil Murphy got wind of the Tucker Carlson interview and instructed the local police not to let us in the building on Monday morning. We were constantly being fed information from inside the government throughout the fight, this was the first of many tips we would get. Laughing at the futility of this move, we locked ourselves in the gym on Sunday evening along with family, friends, members, and volunteers.

Sunday night was filled with emotions, we were all anxious. The gym was filled with people working, trying to get some sleep, and peering out the covered windows. As night turned to morning, you could hear the crowd gathering outside. The noise outside grew from a few voices chanting and talking to a roaring crowd. We peeked out the window and saw that the cavalry had arrived. The parking lot was filled with cars, news vans, and people supporting us at 4 am. All you could see was people cheering and chanting, signs showing support, American flags waving, and news crews setting up.

Our fears were many, we had no idea what to expect but looking out at the parking lot that morning my biggest fears settled. I knew that this fight would be impossible to do alone, this would be a battle where we would need all the help we could get. Our doors were not even open yet and people were ready to go to war with us.

Still, questions loomed...

Would we get arrested?

How would the local and state government react?

Would people come to work out?

What would happen to them?

It was time. My phone rang, it was Pete Hegseth from Fox News. He said he was outside the front door, and he wanted to give us an opportunity to talk to the world. He had driven down from NYC to cover the story and fought to cover the story, instead of leaving it to the local Fox channel.

With a first pump and a deep breath, we took the chains off the inside of the doors and flung them open to see what was waiting for us. In all the chaos, one thing stood out above everything else, the line wrapped around the building all the way to the back of the building. They were ready to stand with us, risk arrest, and fight for freedom by the simple act of walking into the gym to workout.

The day flew by, we were tremendously busy. The feeling was surreal, we were really doing this. The gym was exploding with energy. After 8 weeks of being locked in their homes, hearing nothing but doom and gloom, people were smiling, happy, and laughing. It was like nothing I had ever seen - we were free. The phone was ringing off the hook, and our social media and email were blowing up with words of support and people asking if they drove to the gym would they be able to work out. The line never died down outside the entire day, the parking lot never emptied, and the cameras stayed rolling all day.

The local police were present and originally were a neutral party. The captain said they were on location to make sure everyone was safe. At around noon, there was a commotion outside, someone yelled that the police were approaching. We went outside to a crowd of unhappy supporters. They thought the police were moving in to shut us down. I was able to quiet the crowd down and we stood there waiting for what the police had to say. The captain spoke.

"...you are all in violation of the executive order."

And with a finger in the air before anyone could react.

"On that note. Have a great day. Everybody be safe."

The crowd erupted with a celebration of hugging and cheering. Our people had spoken, and the message was that all businesses were essential – we were not shutting down. It was a truly incredible moment. We had learned that if we come together collectively, We the People are powerful.

Within minutes, the clip of the police standing down was seen by millions online. The phones rang even more than they were, and messages came through every channel by the hundreds. People were calling us asking how to get involved, if they could come to donate cleaning supplies, asking if they drove from another state could they come to work out and support us. There were calls where older men and women were crying and thanking us for what we were doing – many veterans and grandparents. The crowd outside had swelled to hundreds, and the police officers agreed with us. We were gaining momentum. It was clear we were on the right side of this.

It was a nice moment, but also a short-lived one. In the eyes of our state government, we had just done the unspeakable. We had defied them. Murphy had the order down to the police station that they were to get in there and shut us down or there would be consequences for the department. Fifteen minutes later the second in command of the Bellmawr Police came to our door again, to hand us our first of many citations - we would accumulate over eighty between the two of us before this was over. With the music blaring, the weights banging, and the phones ringing we went right back to business.

If it was war they wanted, it was war they would get. We would stay open. No matter what.

CHAPTER 7:

THE ESCALATION AND THE OUTCOME

"We shall defend our island, whatever
the cost may be, we shall fight on the
beaches, we shall fight on the landing
grounds, we shall fight in the fields and
in the streets, we shall fight in the
hills; we shall never surrender."
— **Winston Churchill**

DEFIANT GYM OWNERS V. GOVERNOR PHIL MURPHY

The message we sent to the New Jersey government by reopening was simple:

What you are doing is not fair. It is destructive to our economy, mental health, children's education, and more. Come talk to us. We have a plan; it is a good one. We can be open and still provide safety to our customers and community. We will prove it to you. Come talk anytime.

I think we both understood that Governor Phil Murphy and his cronies were not interested in talking with us. His rhetoric during his news conferences was demeaning. We were brushed off as "defiant gym owners" – a term that became one of endearment. The fact of the matter was, we were making him look stupid and we would continue to do so. In the Governor's press conference on the day of our opening, he made a comment to the head of the State Police about how we should expect increased police presence and interaction in the following days.

What would follow next would be a series of escalations, beginning with the Governor's order to increase police engagement in the following days.

THE FIRST WEEK.

After the success of the first day, energy and anxiety levels were high for all of us. There were so many questions, and nobody knew what was going to happen tomorrow. People slept out in the parking lot that evening guarding the building. There was much to be done to prepare and many problems to solve before the next day. Some of those were major, like what the governor was going to do tomorrow, and some were minor, like needing more ink to print more sign-in slips and paper towels because we were so busy.

It was all hands on deck. We had help pouring in from everywhere – family, friends, members, and people from the local community. It was humbling to see the amount and the ferocity of the support. It came from every corner of the country, every age and background. People went to great lengths to help us. What touched me the most was that none of them wanted anything from us – they were volunteering their time, energy, and money to the cause because they believed it was worth fighting for. This would happen for two years, as the fight to stay open raged on.

The second day started off like the first. The news crews and supporters were still out in the lot, the line of gym-goers got longer, the phones rang even more, and the story of two defiant gym owners standing against COVID tyranny was all over the national news. The police presence escalated, and they began to harass members as they walked in and out of the facility. As the police presence and pressure increased, so did the hostility towards them. The crowd was difficult to keep calm, but they were, until the police arrested a man who had just left the gym for refusing to give his name. Videos of the police putting a handcuffed man in the back of an SUV for the crime of exercising immediately went viral.

The entire world was watching, as the officers conducted the Governor's tyrannical orders. We were gaining more support with every passing minute. We received citations again that day, as did some of our members. The gym stayed open, and nobody was leaving.

Before we could open on the third day, I had to make a public statement. Journalists had dug up the details of the automobile accident almost fifteen years prior and began to write articles portraying me as a dangerous felon who had not learned his lesson. The phones rang with screaming strangers telling us how we were killing people. The comments sections were flooded with hateful messages directed towards me. I put out a video on social media explaining the details of my accident and the statement that what we were doing was bigger than me, and that my mistakes of the past bore no weight on the gym. With a deep breath, I clicked send and the show went on. There was no time for my feelings to be hurt by people I did not know; we were in the fight of our lives. More citations were written that day - nobody cared. The police had set up a camera in the parking lot and were following cars home to pull them over and harass them – so we had the camera removed because it was a violation of private property. Our landlord was hands-off through all this, though he may not have agreed with us on everything, he dealt with the blowback from much of what we were doing and eventually got citations himself from the township. During his daily COVID press conference the governor once again addressed our gym, saying that the Health Department would have to get involved. Coincidentally, our sewage system backed up that day with photos circulating the internet of the township water department trucks in the back of our lot. The official story was they were getting ducks that had fallen into the storm drains.

It is also worth noting that a special shout-out to the New Jersey State Police is due. They were suited up and ready to come in full force to our facility on the third day, but upon being told where they had to go, they outright refused. They were the only government agency to turn down the order to shut our gym down.

The health department pulled up to our building to slap a "Notice of Embargo" on our door around midnight that night. Since there was a sewage mess to clean anyway, we closed on Thursday to reopen on Friday. The media was in a frenzy over our story, I reappeared on Tucker and dozens of other local and national pieces. It felt like there was an army growing behind us, and there was.

It was mostly the same when we reopened on Friday, and it felt like a normal day. We got more citations, but they started sending them to our attorneys because we kept smiling outside and taking pictures with them – unintimidated by the threats of court. Later that night, the governor would go in front of a judge and ask for a court order to have us closed. He would be granted that request and immediately ordered the Sheriff's Department to change the locks on our gym – the one we were still paying rent for, without charging members.

Things were heating up.

THE FIRST MONTH.

With the doors locked, our plan was to let the courts handle the dispute. We made our statement in our protest and as much as we did not like being closed, we tried to approach this fight with as much respect for the system as we could afford.

We turned it over to the courts and the Judicial Branch, to offer some balance to an out-of-control Executive Branch.

Not that it will come as a surprise reading this, but the courts let us down horribly. We had filed in federal court and the judge refused to hear our case on the grounds that we had pending criminal charges in the state we were suing. The truth is, he kicked us back into the controlled and biased courts of the state because nobody wanted to touch this case.

On June 16th, we were granted a motion to reopen because the nutrition store inside was deemed essential and were told not to operate inside. We picked the locks earlier and were already back inside anyway, but this was a small victory. With multiple court cases already pending and a promise that we would have our day in court, it was decided we would operate outside in the parking lot every day - in the interest of being reasonable with the government. In the dog days of summer, when the black top was scorching, we moved 40,000 pounds of weight and machines outside every morning and back inside every night. Our support never stopped. Hundreds of people were showing up to work out in the parking lot every day. We even named the zone the AMAZ (the Anti-Murphy Autonomous Zone) to make fun of the Seattle Antifa CHAZ (Capitol Hill Autonomous Zone) in the wake of the BLM riots. We started our own paper contract tracing system, keeping track of who and how many people came to the gym each day with the intent to prove – if necessary, in a court of law – that we were not getting people sick. We did all this, and they still gave us more citations for not having the proper zoning permission to use the parking lot to workout. The evidence continuously mounted, and it was clear that our government was not acting in the interest of health, but instead, sought complete control. The news was all over it again. As our story grew, we showed no signs of stopping our resistance.

THE FIRST 6 MONTHS.

As the battle against the state entered its third month, we did everything possible to be reasonable and discuss terms to reopen New Jersey businesses immediately. The New Jersey government showed that they were not interested in compromise and the strategy was to punish us into submission.

We were getting nowhere in court - it was delay after delay and then loss after loss. Court was being held on Zoom, and we were not permitted to speak on our own behalf. So, on July 4th we thought it would be a wonderful day to get arrested and we ceased the parking lot gym operations. We made an announcement that the gym was reopening inside again, all were welcome, and no masks would be required. As the government continued to show us, they were unwilling to compromise, we became firmer in what we knew was true. In this case, it was clear masking was not only ineffective but stupid. Citations rolled in, but the show went on. The gym was back open in complete defiance of all lockdown orders, and the facility was packed every day from open to close.

Upon returning to inside operations, we were served with paperwork informing us that we were being charged with Contempt of Court. In proper fashion with the state, we were served with a last-minute notification about a court date just a few days later. It was clear that the judge and court had a favorite, and our gym was not it. The latest request by the governor was to have our doors forcibly locked again and to impose fines on the gym - both were granted.

There were a handful of businesses around the country fighting to stay open. We were all in different states and municipalities, with governors employing unique tactics to shut businesses down. We did our best to help and support each other and sometimes meant a phone call where we would listen to what was happening in each of our respective battles. I spoke to Lou Uridel out in LA County, who was still actively fighting to keep his gym open. Upon telling him the courts had ruled to lock our doors for the second time, he quickly replied, "...take them off. They cannot lock you out if there are no doors."

I laughed, then thought seriously about it. He was right. Moments later our doors were coming off and being sent to a location away from the gym. To this day, it still makes me laugh when I think about the absurdity of it. We had to take the doors off our own business to prevent the government from forcibly closing us down. This is exactly what we wanted to show the world – how unreasonable and out of touch these people were. The doors were off, the gym was now open 24/7 until further notice. Nobody would lock our doors again.

With the gym open and running at capacity every day, we spent our days working and preparing for whatever problems were ahead. Once the doors came off, neither of us left the facility except on rare occasions – our families dealt with it and came to spend time with us. A few days later, under the cover of early morning darkness, the Camden County Sheriffs moved in to arrest us. This was difficult to swallow and a hard truth I had to learn to accept. The cops were not our friends. They were acting as enforcers of the state, and thus failed in their promise to protect American citizens. We had shown support for the police through this entire process and many cops were among the people coming to work out every day. Our member-base was very much the type of people who supports the police.

We walked out in cuffs, arrested for opening our business – for free. Nobody had gotten sick, not one outbreak. But in the eyes of the people who ran our state, we were outlaws. We went peacefully.

Unfortunately for the state, the gym was not empty as it appeared. The whole incident was caught on film by someone in the parking lot who immediately uploaded it on the internet. The media and people all over the country went wild once again. We were showing in real time how out of touch, out of control, and sinister our government was.

The arrest was a charade, and we made a joke of it the entire time. Handcuffed to benches we managed to steal our phones back and were going live on social media from the holding area and talking to the cops through the Ring camera as they figured out how to close the gym. Because there were no doors at the facility, they resorted to covering the doorway by screwing plywood to the frame. Meanwhile back at the station, it took the police more than an hour to figure out what they were charging us with.

We had not broken any laws. Disobeying the executive order had no tangible punishment as it had never really been done before and because mandates are not laws. There we sat, criminals for exercising our right to be free. We were released upon booking. With smiles on our faces, we headed back to the gym to assess the situation. There was no way a couple of sheets of plywood was going to keep us from opening our gym back up. We took a few days off to collect ourselves and prepare for what would come of our next escalation. I would go back on 'Tucker Carlson' that evening and the footage of the two New Jersey gym owners getting arrested was seen by millions of Americans.

Nobody was arrested at Walmart for shopping, yet we were in the thick of an escalating battle with the state because our business was deemed unsafe while others were told they were safe – with not a shred of evidence or data to back those nonsensical distinctions between essential and non-essential. At this time, the State of New Jersey was witnessing a crisis in the nursing homes where thousands of vulnerable individuals were dying after Governor Murphy made the decision to put sick people into nursing homes instead of hospitals. New Jersey suffered some of the highest rates of death in these facilities as a direct result of that choice. Yet there we were, the two defiant gym owners being criminally charged even though we had no problem keeping anyone safe.

I took to social media the next day to officially announce that we would be kicking the plywood down on August 1st and invited members and supporters to join us, because the gym would immediately be open for our community to use.

A day prior, we broke into the gym ahead of time by sawing through the plywood covering. If we just kicked the plywood in, it would destroy the frame and blow the glass out. In broad daylight, in the middle of COVID madness and shutdowns, we squeezed in between the cuts in the plywood and scoped out the inside. Like a scene out of the movies, the cops pulled into the parking lot and circled the gym on patrol. We hit the ground and crawled behind some equipment and shelving. What a ridiculous moment – two grown men breaking into their own business, evading police patrols, and laughing hysterically. Once we lost the heat, we went to work loosening what we had to, so we would not blow the front of our building out kicking down the plywood. We slipped out undetected, covering our hole in the door with another piece of plywood.

The next day – with a crowded parking lot of members, supporters, and media – we stomped our way through the plywood barricade, walked into the gym, turned the music and lights on, covered the windows back up, and the gym was once again open for all. Every escalation from us or the state provoked the other party to respond with more force. Tensions rose alongside excitement. The state was committed to making us bend to their will no matter what, they had issued dozens of citations, locked our doors, sabotaged our plumbing, issued court orders, arrested not only us but also our members, and boarded up our doors. Their efforts to stop us only made them look worse.

I looked at my phone one day shortly after and I read a text message that said, "Ian, this is Dan Bongino. I want to come to the gym."

I had been a fan of Dan's for a while and had even heard him praise our efforts on his show a few days earlier. He reached out to me on a particularly frustrating day. We had just taken another loss in court. His call was a much-needed gust of wind in our sails. While we were talking, he was getting fired up at the injustice of what was being done to us and small businesses around the country. Dan flew up to New Jersey to get a workout and record his podcast right in the middle of the gym – all in two hours. He put it out on his show the day before and pulled the trigger. The parking lot was full of fresh faces who had come out just because Dan told them to. He greeted and spent time talking to the hundreds of fans who showed up and took pictures with everyone. Immediately after, he jumped right into a full-blown workout. Dan ran around the gym that day in jeans. He proceeded to hammer out a few good sets of everything – heavy deadlifts and dumbbell presses, pullups and dips, speed bag work, and more. He was a sweaty mess in 30 minutes.

As soon as he completed the workout, we sat down to a podcast. We filmed a full show discussing the COVID hysteria, hypocrisy, and our fight to stay open. Support, donations, and T–shirt sales came pouring in immediately from his loyal audience – they were now our supporters too. He hopped back on his plane and made a stop at a tattoo parlor in North Carolina who had stayed open before heading home that day. Dan is an ace, a true patriot. What he did that day helped us gain a massive amount of momentum, adding to our ability to withstand anything the government would do to us.

Dan would be the first influential voice to visit our facility, but dozens more join him throughout the saga. Each time someone new visited the gym, they would share our story to a new network of people. Most of these people did not have businesses that were under attack, but they understood the reality of the situation that impacted all Americans. Our liberties were under attack, and they were able to help by getting the story out. Day after day, our story was talked about on the news and social media feeds all over the world. Our network of friends grew more powerful and effective. Every time the state moved against us; they recruited more people to our side of the fight.

After I finished my third appearance on 'The Tucker Carlson Show,' I opened my phone to see an encouraging message from a guy named Andy Frisella. I knew of him as the co-Founder and CEO of the company 1st Phorm, but besides that, not much. I thanked him for supporting us and sharing our story to his audience of millions. Over the next few days and weeks, we would regularly discuss the insanity in our world. He would check in every day to see what was happening at the gym and was quick to pick up the phone when I needed to blow off some steam. We became close friends overnight. Not only did I get a gritty and truly loyal friend, but I was welcomed into the incredible family of people who work for and use 1st Phorm products – overnight, our gym had tens of thousands of new allies.

There are a couple hundred more people that I have had the pleasure of connecting with. A simple lesson we learned early on, when you do good things, good people find you.

The state showed no willingness to diffuse the situation and neither did we. As the media on both sides covered the story it was clear nobody was backing down. This would go on until one of us could not continue. The governor and his attorney general would go right back to court looking for more punishment levied against us. Before August was over the courts decided to levy a $15,497.76/day fine against us – for every day that we remained open. $15,497.76 a day for being open when we were not even charging our members, and nobody was getting sick. If we were charging our members, we would be taking in about $30,000 a month in memberships – before we paid all the overhead. It was clear that the only objective of the state was to put us out of business once and for all. After they formally began levying fines against the gym, they subpoenaed all our business and personal financial accounts.

Andy said something to me during this time that had stuck with me through the years. It illustrates why it is so important to help others when a wrong is being done to them. I called him one day when I was in a particularly dark place. I was broken, scared, it felt like they were going to take everything. The fines broke a hundred thousand and were quickly piling up to a million. I was so mad I was in tears. I screamed into the phone, and he just listened. When I was done, he told me that I needed to keep going and that all I needed to worry about was opening the gym. He promised he would come out of his own pocket to make sure we would survive this and to pretend the fines do not exist. If we had to pay, he would not leave us to carry the burden alone. I asked why he cared and why he would do something like that. He said he was not stupid enough to think that after they were done with me, they were not going to come for him and his business. I laughed, but he was right. Unfortunately, at the time this was something most people did not realize – and many still do not. Most people will watch an injustice because it is not happening directly to them – it is easier that way.

Murphy was successfully using the biased state courts against us. The judge on our case was up for tenor that year, as they are appointed in New Jersey, not elected. It was clear he was going to make another attempt to physically close us down. He went back to court and requested a metal barricade be erected - because the wooden one clearly was not sufficient. We scrambled for another solution, my partner was prepared to chain himself to the railing and stopped eating for days in preparation. I called the one politician who had said he wanted to help the gym. He was not an elected official, but he was running for Senate. I met Rik Mehta earlier at the first reopening rally I spoke at and attended. We stayed connected, and he frequently pledged to help us when we could find a way. That time had come. We did some homework and found out that political offices were exempt from all COVID-19 executive orders. Within days the gym was declared to be an official Rik Mehta for Senate volunteer location, where people could get campaign information, sign up to volunteer, and get connected with others. We announced on the news, alongside Rik, that it would now be election interference to close our gym. Governor Phil Murphy's executive order was now meaningless. After spending more than 40 days open 24/7 with no doors and living at the gym, we were able to put the doors back on and sleep in our own beds.

That month ended with one more blow from the state. The township was pressured to hold a special meeting about the gym. The meeting was another sham and the town council members voted to revoke our business license by stating that our gym was a danger to the community. When asked for proof of that danger, a town council member replied that customers of the neighboring dollar store were concerned for their health. Coincidentally, after our license was revoked, Governor Murphy allowed gyms to reopen just 3 days later. We ceased being fined for being open, but the Attorney General filed another motion in the court to compel us to sign an affidavit swearing that we would mandate masks. If not, the fine of $15,497.76 daily would resume. When you are faced with a choice like that, you discover how strong your convictions are and what you are made of. They were threatening us with catastrophic fines for not mandating masks. All we had to do was say that we would enforce it, and they would stop. But we knew that if we bent the knee, even slightly, they would hang us on it. Our principles were more powerful than the punishment.

Fuck you.

No deal.

Fines or no fines, we were staying open.

License or no license, we were staying open.

THE FIRST YEAR.

As our fight continued, we settled into a routine. Once most of the fireworks went off, most of the action was what was going back and forth in the courts. Getting tied up in the courts was expensive and slow. Not only that, but they have essentially unlimited funding, and you are playing in their courts. Businesses in lockdown states like New Jersey, were being allowed to reopen under other restrictions like mask mandates and vaccine requirements but our gym was still "shut down." When they took our business license, we laughed it off and continued to operate as we had been. We were not charging anybody anyway, we called ourselves a recreation center and continued to ignore any pressure to shut down. It was long hours, 7 days a week at the gym. The foot traffic was incredible, we were doing 500-800 visitors a day, often more. And we were still being fined daily.

Several months after the fines began, we walked into work one morning to discover that our business bank account had been completely wiped out – over $170,000 was confiscated by the state. The money in those accounts was from donations and people buying t-shirts that were raised to fight our ongoing legal battles and to keep the gym open. After I learned that the state had stolen our money, I put out another update video on social media. I told the world what they had done and that despite having no money, we would not be closing – the gym was open, we would figure it out. The video went viral and yet again people from all over the country decided they were going to help. Over the next week $100,000 in T-shirt orders came through, on top of donations. There were a lot of moments like this throughout those days and I focused on enjoying them. Despite all the injustice that was happening to us, good people continuously blessed us. The strength and resources to stand back up after getting knocked down repeatedly was given to us by other people.

When we reopened, we did not have more than a few pieces of basic apparel. However, when reopening turned into a long-drawn-out battle, people wanted to get involved with more than a donation. People wanted to represent our gym – wearing a shirt from the gym became a statement against lockdowns and mandates and a symbol of freedom and liberty. What started as one small rack of shirts turned into a full-blown operation with dozens of colors, designs, and apparel choices. As we were ending the first year, it became clear this fight was going to drag on. Our supporters made it clear they were here to stay, and gym apparel became the way that people contributed memberships, guest passes, or a way for people from around the U.S. and eighteen different countries to support from a distance.

With encouragement also came criticism. The difference was that the critics never stayed around. When the gym was on the news, the critics would harass us, but it was never long before most of them had moved onto the next thing they were supposed to be outraged about. Meanwhile, we had visitors coming to the gym from all over. On any given day we had people dropping in from out of state visiting NJ to come workout, take a picture, or just see the gym and chat with us for a bit. I am certain we had someone from all fifty states come to the gym and most of our members were traveling up to 45 minutes to come - even after other gyms were allowed to reopen - because they believed in the importance of our stand against tyranny. The energy was unmatched in the gym, and we kept rolling with the punches.

After our 50,000th 'COVID free' check-in, you would think at least one government or health official would be interested in learning about our safety protocol. Not a word. When we reached our 100,000th 'COVID free' check-in at the gym in January 2021, the media was reporting that an Amazon warehouse had 20,000+ COVID positive workers. There was no outcry, no shutdown of any of their warehouses, yet, our gym, with proven statistics, was being targeted. They could not seem to slow the spread and stop people from getting sick. According to their own press conferences and policies, people were spreading the virus and dying at an alarming rate. Yet at the gym, everyone was happy and healthy. The lockdowns were never about your health.

The whole purpose behind the contact tracing system and tally of total visits was to prove them wrong and make them look stupid. As we hit significant numbers, we would make another video and show the world. The stack of paperwork grew larger and more laughable with each day. Where were all the people who were supposed to be getting sick because the gym was open?

As the first year of "fourteen days to flatten the curve" came to an end, it was clear that there was a long road ahead. We had litigation in multiple courts – municipal for our 80+ Bellmawr Police Department citations, suing the township for our business license in state court, fighting civil contempt of court charges and fines brought against us in another state court, and lastly fighting criminal contempt of court charges brought against us in the criminal division.

THE SECOND YEAR.

Whenever you take on a big entity like the state or a corporation, it is expected that you will endure heavy losses in court and in your wallet. Legal battles are costly and can be drawn out by lawyers to make them even more painful. The cost to prepare a single argument, write the motion, and appear in court is often $30,000 or more with a legal team that knows what they are doing. We would spend well over half a million dollars in legal bills just fighting to stay open. The state was spending taxpayer money to fight us in court, while we relied on the generosity of our members and supporters around the country. As a business that was not charging its customers, not allowed to charge its customers, had its bank accounts emptied, and was constantly under attack from a hostile government, we were able to make it work – somehow, someway, the fight went on.

In that David v. Goliath, Rocky Balboa, underdog story, it is a twelve-round fight, and the good guys get their heads bashed in rounds one through eleven. Going up against these kinds of people, you are sure to be demonized, they will try to bankrupt you, break your spirits, threaten you, will not play fair, and the cards are stacked against you. But the fight is to be had, nonetheless. It was the second year of being open against lockdowns, and though the government had lifted lockdowns they were moving into vaccine mandates. We were still tangled up in the New Jersey courts, operating like a rogue command center.

Our focus remained the same, our business would never close or adhere to any form of government tyranny – including vaccine mandates. We kept the business model of a free recreation center that was open to the public, and if you wanted to contribute or donate in any way that was appreciated. Almost everyone did, and generously. We still had the nutrition store running and that was helpful, people would go out of their way to shop there. What had started as a couple of people requesting T-shirts had grown into a full-blown apparel company. People donated their time regularly to help clean the gym and keep it running smoothly.

Collectively, we were unstoppable. We truly defied all the odds – a free gym that was able to stay open and not only pay our typical overhead, but also the increased cost of cleaning and other supplies while financing a massive legal battle against the state.

There was much less chaos at the gym during the second year than the first. Once Governor Phil Murphy had his grip on us in the court system, he stopped bothering with the police and other attempts to shut us down. Court was easier for the state, it made for less media and provided fewer chances to make them look stupid. It was easy for them to hide in the middle of drawn-out court battles instead of giving ammunition for our gym to be on the news every week.

The calm allowed us to focus on continuing to build an amazing facility, host powerlifting meets, use the brand we created to help others with political rallies, and organize charity efforts. It was a fun time. The energy and the feeling of family at the gym had only intensified. The gym was the most normal place on earth for a lot of people – we did not require any of the masks or vaccines, and we did not judge anyone who chose to. The gym was so diverse, and it all worked beautifully – no matter who anyone was, we all agreed on the concept that people should be free to make their own choices and not be pressured by anyone to do something they did not want to do.

What a novel concept.

Using COVID as an excuse, the court system was perverted by using Zoom hearings to hold court – this is not a legitimate way to hold any serious proceedings. Our microphones were always muted, and we were forced to just sit and listen to whatever punishment the judge would decide. Not once were we permitted our right to speak on our own behalf in court. Our legal system has been broken for a long time, but the COVID shenanigans proved just how much of a joke most of our judicial system really is.

Late in 2021, we were moved from the Bellmawr Municipal court to the Winslow Township Municipal court because our lawsuit against the town created a conflict of interest in the matter of all the local citations. Eighteen months after reopening, we had not been inside a courtroom, but to our surprise, our hearing was being held in-person. This was unexpected, as New Jersey was one of the last states to drop restrictions and COVID measures.

We went to court that day fully expecting to be arrested. We were not going to wear a mask in the building, as we had drawn a hard line in the sand a long time ago. The court officers recognized us and initially told us we would need masks. We refused, politely. One of the officers said he was not surprised and that he would be right back. Upon returning, he said the Judge did not care if we wore masks, and to go wait in the courtroom with everyone else.

It was common for a lot of people – state employees or otherwise – to commend us for what we were doing. These officers chatted with us for a while, talking about our fight, how they respected us for what we were doing, and how they disagreed with how the Governor was handling the situation. This was not a bad start to our day, considering we had expected to get turned around at the door. We even had bail money on us, just in case.

New venue, new judge, new prosecutor. This could be a good thing; it could not be any worse than what we had been through. As we watched the judge interact with others in the courtroom, it became clear that this was the most reasonable judge we had encountered. She was pleasant with all, spoke in a positive manner and worked with both sides of every case to come to the best conclusions for all parties.

A sense of ease came over me as we were called to the stand. We were there for a pre-trial conference, which is on the record but is not a formal proceeding in prosecution. This was the first opportunity to look at the case and get a read on what all sides wanted to do. She asked if we could all talk casually on the matter at hand.

Not only was this our first opportunity to be heard, but it was in a manner that was open and receptive. It felt as close to fair and impartial as one could get. It was obvious by her reaction that she was confused how the state had taken such dramatic actions against us. Even the prosecutor in the municipal court was open and wanted to hear what we had to say for ourselves. Neither judge nor the prosecutor knew what to do with the messy file that accompanied our case. After a year and a half of losing, having no ability to speak, and being punished harshly, this was our first experience with any type of justice.

We explained how our business was shut down without anyone coming in to see the extensive protocols we set up for safety. We showed that we recently passed our 280,000th 'COVID free' check-in – with the paperwork to prove it. We explained the extensive list of actions the state took against our business.

The judge was taken back by the details, she had questions as to why there were so many tickets against us, who took our business license and how, why we were fined such an intentionally destructive amount of money, and more.

The dialogue continued for several minutes. It was incredible to be heard. There was much more to discuss on the matter, but we were thankful that this woman viewed the courtroom as the people's courtroom – not hers. She was humble, kind, and understanding. That hearing gave me reassurance that there was a light at the end of the tunnel. I left that day feeling relieved.

Around the same time, we had our pleasant meeting with the municipal judge, the Attorney General of New Jersey brought seven criminal charges of Contempt of Court against us. This was unexpected because these charges were for what had happened a year earlier, when we took the doors off and kicked in the plywood. Surprising, but nobody was shocked. We had come to expect a clown show from the state. It appeared that Phil Murphy only cared about hurting the two defiant gym owners for making him look like a fool during the lockdowns. These charges added more legal bills and we were already spread thin through several courts. Fighting this was going to be expensive and challenging to win. This was a good move on their part, we were late deep into this fight and had limited resources. If found guilty we faced up to 4.5 years in prison for the charges.

January of 2022, we made the choice to accept the guilty plea on one charge instead of wasting resources attempting to fight them. This was a move I was heavily criticized for by some, who felt like we were submitting to the system. Most failed to understand that it would have depleted our already sparse financial resources. The problem was these charges were based on the claim that we defied the judge's order to stay closed - which is illegal. We openly defied this order. For the courts, this was a straightforward case. The question of, "Was the judge's order lawful?" is not a factor in these charges. To prove our innocence, we would have to fight the judge's court order (which we already were) and that would take months, if not years to get it overturned. It was easier to take the guilty plea for a slap on the wrist and keep focused on where we had the chance to win.

Our sentencing was another one of those inspiring and humbling moments. People from the gym, the community, and the country rallied to support us. The Zoom server that allowed people to watch crashed within minutes because too many people were on it. The judge received hundreds of messages and letters on our behalf. Many of those letters detailed why the writer thought it was so important our gym had stayed open – there were personal testimonies about how our efforts had helped them with PTSD, suicide, addiction, depression, confidence, and improve health issues because of what we did. The judge was impressed by the support and gave us the minimum sentence for our plea. We agreed to plead guilty to "taking the doors off of our business" in violation of a court order to shut our facility down. Our punishment was one year of probationary supervision. I have been in trouble most of my life in some form or another, but this was a joke. Nobody sick, nobody dying, yet we were being treated like criminals because we exposed the hypocrisy and lies of our governor. Take the hit and keep moving.

As we approached the end of our second year battling the state, the pace of the fight slowed to a crawl. The litigation moves slowly – 30 days for this motion, 30 days for a reply, 30 days for a date to be set, and so on. We were taking our losses and filing our appeals – just like our lawyer had told us from the onset. We were warned that when you challenge the system, the system does not play fair. "Expect to lose, until you win," was the warning he gave.

Battle fatigue had set in at this stage. Reopening the gym came with a heavy cost. There was a tremendous amount of stress, anxiety, frustration, weariness, and fear that came with taking on the government. We worked every day and rarely had any time off. This was a cost many people paid, not just the owners. Our families and friends sacrificed their time with us through the ups and downs of the rollercoaster. The state used its entire arsenal against us, and we were still standing firm in our opposition to COVID mandates.

VINDICATION.

As year two came to a close, we achieved a major victory. After the revocation of our business license, we sued the township. We initially lost and were now working our way through the appeals process. The COVID narrative was falling apart at this point, only the Federal Government and deep blue states were still holding onto their mandates and restrictions. Even diehard COVID loonies were losing their enthusiasm for the restrictions.

In our appeal, we had subpoenaed township emails because it was obvious they were pressured to revoke our license. In those records, we discovered that they had never actually taken away our business license like they said they did. However, they issued us dozens of citations for 'Operating without a business license.' After turning over these records to us, the mayor and town council rushed to take our license – a strange misstep on their part. Just like that, we finally had something to work with in this case.

At the same time, the township asked our attorneys how long we planned to pursue legal action against them – as if they had expected us to give up. The response was simple. Until we get our business license reinstated, at minimum. We had resubmitted for a license once before with no answer and did it again. Shortly after, two brand new business licenses for our gym and nutrition shop came in the mail. The township had folded its hand. We caught them in a lie, and they knew it. We never got an official explanation, but I assume they could no longer justify the expense of the court battle to taxpayers and because they knew they had messed up in not taking it, citing us, and then taking it away a year later. The truth is, I did not care then and do not care now. We won. Our gym was never successfully shuttered by the local, county, or state government, despite their best attempts to do so. For two long years we stood our ground and the enemy had finally begun to retreat. Effective immediately, the gym would be running like a normal business again. We were regular business owners again. There were more battles in court to be fought, but this was by far the most important victory. The gym remained open through the storm.

We had held the wolves at bay, inspired a nation of people to do the same in their own ways and successfully navigated a resistance against bad governing.

Within the first week of resuming normal billing, we had almost a thousand members signed up. It felt good to be back to normal. All that remained was our municipal charges and appeals on the fines, but until then, it was back to business.

NOT A TWO-MAN ARMY.

If two gym owners from New Jersey had opened their doors and nobody came out to support them, we would have been sitting in a jail cell and had our doors closed by the end of the day. One of the parts of this story I enjoyed the most is the diversity of people who contributed to our fight. We drew support from all ages and backgrounds because what we were doing was not political, it was the right thing to do. I had the pleasure of meeting thousands, reading messages from tens of thousands, and speaking in front of hundreds of thousands. Our strength to get through the challenges was a result of the smiles, donations, prayers, hugs, stories, words of encouragement, and more.

To the original and new members, the parking lot protestors, the guests from around the country, the people who donated and bought apparel from across the country and around the world, the people who prayed and sent letters and messages, the people on social media who shared updates relentlessly, and to the media members who made our reopening an international story for two years - thank you.

To our families, thank you. The truth is none of you had a choice in what we did. The shutdowns wound up on our doorstep and were going to fight them regardless. There was a great deal of personal sacrifice and criticism you had to put up with by being our family. I was absent when it came to helping others during this time, especially my close family. The fight to stay open was consuming. My wife had many hospital visits alone because I was at the gym, a speaking engagement, or not able to enter the hospital because of my public stance on masks. Being in the hospital is not a pleasant experience and without someone to be next to you, it is worse. This is one example of many - both families and friend circles suffered.

The beauty of this story is that it was an organic movement. We never knew the fight would be as big as it would become, but we held firm in our convictions, even as it got scary. What started as a small group of COVID outlaws, spread into a national movement of COVID resistance that was joined by millions. That small network of supporters grew in stride with the escalating battle with the state. Every time something bad happened to us, our friends and supporters rallied to make sure that we could stay standing in our defiance. I do not think you can get a better example behind the power of "We the People..." than something like this.

CHARITY AMONG CHAOS.

From the time we took over the gym, one of our core values was charity. We wanted our business to become a part of the community. Even amid the chaos of fighting the state of New Jersey, we were able to use the influx in foot traffic to our gym to give back as much as we could to people in need.

It started with our second annual food drive, which we had done before the lockdowns. Our first year, there was an impressive haul of food, about a pickup truck's worth. When we ran the food drives during the lockdowns, we produced triple what we had on our original food drive. Our members were stepping over boxes of food for weeks to get into the gym during our efforts. Our food drives went so well that we jumped at the opportunity to help around Christmas too. This is a trend many businesses follow, and for good reason. We wanted to make it bigger, not just a box or two of toys, but truckloads of them. I contacted Chris, a friend through 1st Phorm and an NYPD officer who held an annual toy drive gym event in previous years. We agreed to host the event at the gym and 1st Phorm stepped up by sponsoring the toy drive. Both times we held the event, we filled a box truck and school bus with toys. A picture does not do it justice.

Then came VOW 2021. A day to remember.

Veterans Outreach Workout was an event that had been running for 5 years at Warhouse Gym. The event was organized by New Jersey veteran Phil Dore, hosted by Rob and Dana

Bailey at their facility. After the closure of Warhouse Gym, we volunteered to host it in August 2021.

The goal of the event was simple: bring the fitness community together in honor of the men and women who sacrifice to serve our country and raise money for veteran charities. We wanted to go as big as possible and make sure the event was a tremendous success. We were in the middle of COVID and our fight with the government, so we did not bother pulling any permits or asking permission to host an event. With no idea where to start, I spoke to Phil and Rob about how the event worked in the past. I asked Rob what he was most proud of and what he would have done differently. Rob answered honestly and said that the events had always been incredible, but he wished they had raised more money to donate. We set out to keep that one-of-a-kind energy they created with VOW and aimed to be able to write some big checks for three veteran charities at the end. We selected Paws and Warriors, Adopt a Cop BJJ, and FitOps.

I began reaching out to all the people who had shown support for our gym in the fitness industry. People were immediately receptive, anyone with a fan-base or following in the fitness industry could donate to the event just by coming and dozens of them did on their own dime. I announced that we would be hosting the event and asked all businesses who wanted to participate to reach out. We did not want to leave anyone out, so we worked with every business to make sure they contributed to the event in some way – be that with free giveaways, sponsorship, or a percentage of any sales they made. Every business that attended contributed beyond what I had asked. Consistent with our efforts to stay open, people's generosity did not fail. Support came from everywhere; people were calling the gym asking if they could help come set up the event and volunteer the day of.

1st Phorm got us started with a huge donation. Recovery CBD, Axe&Sledge, Redcon1, Phonesites, Lions Not Sheep, MDK Project, Mind Pump Media, and dozens of other companies wrote checks, showed up, sent product, brand reps, and more.

We threw it together as best we could and pulled the trigger. That day, a hundred influential fitness professionals and dozens of small and medium sized businesses showed up alongside thousands of attendees. We had people of every discipline running seminars, contests, and spending time with fans – bodybuilding, powerlifting, strongman, MMA, and more.

The day started with a salute to the flag, to the brave men and women who serve this country, some speeches, and the National Anthem. People were everywhere, inside, and outside of the gym. Vendors lined the parking lot. In New Jersey, during COVID, this was a super spreader event, but to us, it was freedom. There were bodies getting tossed around on the mats by our MMA professionals Frankie Edgar, Greg Anderson, and Mitch Aguiar. IFFB Pros getting workouts in with the people they inspire. A deadlift competition rocked the building. A tribute to veterans who have taken their lives with twenty-two pushups on the minute, every minute – led by Navy SEAL veteran Ray Care.

As a result of the generosity of those who donated their time, their money, and effort we raised an initial $75,000 for the three charities and thousands more in the following weeks as we continued to sell the leftover T-shirts from the event.

Without a doubt, this was one of the most memorable events of the last few years. I stood on the catwalk above the gym leaning over the railing, looking down onto the packed facility with pride. It was not the first or the last time the gym would explode with energy like this, but this one was special. We successfully pulled off Veterans Outreach Workout 2021. As we were being fined $15k daily, we were helping our community. What was the government doing for people in need?

CHAPTER 8:

OUTSIDE THE GYM

"Each time a man stands up for an ideal,
or acts to improve the lot of others,
or strikes out against injustice, he
sends forth a tiny ripple of hope."
- Robert F Kennedy.

THE TRUTH IS EASY TO TELL.

When the media came with questions, we always had an answer. There was never hesitation in our voices, we believed in what we were doing and knew what was happening to Americans was wrong. We had done our research and took it seriously. Before reopening, we set out to have as much of an understanding of COVID as possible. It is easy to speak on matters when you are telling the truth and it is easy to be probed with questions when you have done your homework. If you look back at the way public officials spoke during the lockdowns, you can tell that they were lying. There was no conviction in the voices of the politicians, but we spoke with authority and confidence on all questions - and over three years since the start of COVID, we have been proved right about everything we said.

Small business owners who spoke out across the country regularly made politicians look stupid on national television. Governor Phil Murphy appeared on Tucker Carlson making a bumbling statement about not considering the constitution in his actions right around the time we were in front of the cameras speaking passionately and confidently about our right to stay open. The gym reopening coincided with the first major pushback against lockdowns and that small resistance would spread to other forms of protest against COVID tyranny.

After the first Tucker Carlson appearance, speaking in front of the cameras felt natural. I had survived not making a fool out of myself in front of the millions of viewers on that show, so talking to any other camera was no longer intimidating. It was like being thrown in the deep end and finding out I could swim; I became a public speaker overnight.

People were resisting lockdowns all over affected areas of the country. The more people that spoke out, the louder the resistance became. From the moment we opened, the phone rang with requests for me to come speak at other protests, rallies, and events. The first time the phone rang, we were only two weeks into the resistance and our hands were full keeping the gym open, but it felt important that I go speak. We hoped that other businesses would open with us, but very few did. I saw it as vital to continue to get our story out to inspire more people to open, defy mandates, and support and protect small businesses.

I arrived to speak at that first event back in May of 2020 to the sight of a large and energetic crowd, full of American flags. It was great to see so many people, but I knew then that this was only the beginning of a long road. I stood in front of the crowd and received a hero's welcome. As I started to speak, I got nervous, my legs shook, but I stuck to what I knew to be true. What was happening to small businesses was wrong and everyone there agreed. The crowd erupted with cheers as I told them about what my partner and I were going through at the gym and encouraged them to find where they could help and get involved. Because of the severity and intensity of our story, everyone wanted me to come and speak at their events. Hundreds of requests would follow in the next two years.

WORDS MATTER.

COVID became an information war. Most people who did not agree with lockdowns were getting their news from social media and events. As the demand to hear me speak increased, so did my popularity. Throughout the lockdowns regular people – who spoke out – grew massive social media platforms, mine exploded to well over a million followers. My social media functioned as the gym's emergency broadcast network, and we were always able to get information out to the public. Words became weapons to the foundation of lies that lockdown policy was built upon.

"Everything the government is doing right now is designed to make you fat, weak, stupid, depressed, lazy, and reliant on crumbs they wipe off their plates.

Health replaced by pharmaceuticals.

Education replaced by programming.

Hard work replaced by handouts.

These people hate you."

I saw that quote translated into six different languages and it was turned into a graphic that was shared by tens of millions of people. It was something I said at one of my many speaking engagements and tweeted after. I had no idea when I put it out that it would be used as a source of inspiration for many. People were looking for leadership and the only requirements were truth and the courage to speak it, and in the age of cancel-culture and political correctness, many were and still are scared to do so.

Speaking engagements became a regular occasion for me. It served to generate momentum for the gym and lend support to others around the country. Calls came in from all over the country – from Nebraska to Florida, tiny protests to the stage of CPAC and Washington D.C., audiences of a couple dozen to hundreds of thousands. Our gym was not the only battleground, and our influence could also help others. By announcing events and coming to speak, supporters of the gym were able to network with smaller grassroots organizations in their local area. The strategy was simple, if enough people could be inspired, emboldened, assisted, and encouraged to fight back, then the COVID narrative would fall apart. Our gym could not be the only hill people were fighting to defend. The more businesses that opened, the more anti-mandate rallies and protests, the more people who refused to wear masks, the quicker we would get back to normal. The government would not be able to contain the resistance if businesses and citizens all over the country were in defiance – eventually they ran out of people to enforce their lockdown orders. I spoke about this very idea sitting atop a ladder in front of a crowd of hundreds outside of Mac's Public House – a Staten Island bar that defied lockdowns – as the sheriffs stood trying to hold back a huge crowd waiting to go inside. We inspired NYC to stand up and join in on the fight and we would do that all over the country, until so many small fires had been lit that the COVID narrative collapsed.

MOST SECURE ELECTION EVER.

2020 was a wild year, COVID, and the lockdowns were chaotic, confusing, and criminal, but we did not know that COVID was just the setup for what would be the biggest joke of an election that our country has ever seen. The American people supported Donald J. Trump for reelection in awe-inspiring numbers. For months leading up to the presidential election we saw Trump parades with cars, motorcycles, and boats, there were signs everywhere, massive rallies, and constant support in the streets. There are plenty who will dispute this, even to this day, but it was obvious who the country supported at that time.

On election night, we were not given an answer as to who was the winner of the election. We were told of delays from pipes bursting and errors with machines. Videos of misconduct and election interference spread across the internet and Big Tech was quickly on top of it, censoring and banning people for reporting the content showing what was happening in elections throughout several states.

At the time, it was clear that millions of Americans believed the election was stolen from Donald Trump, and they demanded audits and accountability. People mobilized to help "stop the steal." Protests and rallies popped up throughout the country in support of Donald Trump – none more infamous than the DC rallies that eventually lead to the now infamous January 6th rally.

NOVEMBER 13, 2020.

I got the call to come speak on behalf of the President for the first DC Rally and happily agreed. I had watched the election in real time and had strong doubts about the legitimacy of what the American people just witnessed. The drive down to Washington D.C. was something that I will never forget. As I traveled south down I-95 there were more cars on the road flying Trump 2020 flags than there were regular vehicles. Upon arrival, DC was already blocked off and most of the streets were shut down near the city. People were everywhere. There is no way to have gotten a proper head count that day, but I can confidently say it was attended by more than a million. It was electric, people came from all over and were filled with love for their country, president, and fellow countrymen. The streets were shoulder to shoulder near the city center. I walked to Freedom Plaza where the rally was set to begin. After a series of speakers, we were marching to the Supreme Court to show our support of the President and urge the court to act appropriately with the legal questions that had been brought before them.

Freedom Plaza was unreal, there was not an inch of standing room as far as you could see. At one point during the rally Marine One flew overhead with President Trump on board, and the there was a deafening roar from the crowd. It felt like home. I was proud to be a patriot in the crowd and a speaker among the impressive lineup on the stage that day. Standing in front of that massive crowd to speak left an impact and taught me a lesson I strive to live and share daily.

Do not ever tell yourself the lie that you are "just one person" because less than a year earlier I was "just one person" and now I stood before tens of thousands using my voice to inspire them to fight for their country. I was there because we had shown courage at the gym by reopening. What we did is something that we all have the capacity to do. Your whole life can change with one decision to do the right thing. We often underestimate the importance of what we do; we tell ourselves we are insignificant. We are not.

As day turned to night, there was a shift in the energy. Antifa had started to come out as the sun set. Scuffles broke out, elderly men and women were attacked and bullied, and soon Black Lives Matter protests joined alongside the Antifa attacks. In response, large groups of men took to the streets to provide protection to people who were being attacked as they walked to their vehicles or found themselves separated from a group.

The situation continued to escalate as the groups of Antifa and Black Lives Matter came together and squared off with groups of American Flag wielding patriots – unaffiliated, Proud Boys, and other groups. Things got ugly quickly and skirmishes broke out in the streets. Antifa got smashed that evening, it was not even close. Those who have more to fight for, more to protect, and more to lose tend to prevail when it comes down to conflict. Most of the agitators at events like this are paid or incentivized to be there, they did not have a dog in this fight.

DECEMBER 12, 2020.

The second rally on December 12, 2020, was nearly identical to the first with much of the same energy and events. There were less people, but it was not small by any stretch of the imagination. The violence that night was the same as the first rally, but worse. Time was ticking and the efforts to force the government to investigate the election were scrambling to get traction. As we learned during COVID, fighting against the media, big tech companies, and the uniparty was an uphill battle.

JANUARY 6, 2021

The night of January 5th had an entirely different feel than the previous D.C. rallies. I spoke again at Freedom Plaza that evening. It was cold and rainy, but the crowd was once again shoulder to shoulder. The energy was different, this felt like the final hour. People were still full of love and good energy like they had always been, but it felt heavy this time. There was almost no Antifa or Black Lives Matter presence the night before, which was odd and left many feeling concerned. This was set to be the biggest and most important rally concerning 2020's election integrity issues, the evening before Congress was set to certify the election, and they were nowhere to be found. It did not feel right.

It was clear there were paid agitators in the crowd on both January 5th and 6th. People dressed-up in MAGA gear called for violence, when it was made clear this would be a peaceful protest. It was obvious to the crowd who these outsiders were. The protesters in the streets that night were quick to point them out and distance themselves. One of those men was the now notorious Ray Epps, who I ran into at BLM plaza that evening. He was yelling into a microphone about taking the country back and appeared out of place with the rest of the crowd. Numerous people recorded his phony antics on camera that night. He was also seen on the front lines of the barriers coming down at the capitol the next day.

Around this time, there had been a dramatic increase in threats I was receiving. Andy advised strongly that I do not go without private security. I thought it was unnecessary, but I decided to listen to his concerns and hire a detail to watch me. COVID hysteria was still running high, so I was either loved or hated, and those who hated me proved to be unpredictable at times. Unlike the other two rallies, tensions were high during the daytime. People did not know what was going to happen, there were all sorts of calls coming out for people to be prepared to camp outside, hotels with vacancies were denying people rooms, President Trump had requested people to come this time, and the National Guard was told to hold back. Nobody knew what to expect.

On the cold morning of January 6th, I went to meet with my security detail on my way to the Ellipse – where the president was set to speak. It was still early and the size of the crowd in that area was unlike anything I had ever seen before. The Ellipse and the Washington monument are both massive wide-open spaces that total over 150 acres, and it was filling up quickly. It reminded me of the iconic images of the crowd at Woodstock. There were so many people that I could not find my security detail and even if I knew where he was, it would have taken an hour to get to him. The Capitol speakers had seats in the front couple of rows to hear the President, his son Don Jr., and others speak at the ellipse first. Trump spoke for nearly an hour and towards the end of it, the directive was given for the Capitol speakers to start heading towards the event and to get ready. We had an escort through the mobs of people, and I was finally able to connect with my security detail. Under his advice, we chose to break off from the group and head to the Capitol ourselves.

As the Capitol building came into sight, you could hear the crowd chanting and the commotion of another mass of people. Concussion grenades were being thrown into the crowd. I was not sure where we were supposed to be for the speech and was confused by what seemed like offensive placement of grenades into the crowd. We made our way closer to the building and stopped short when we realized there was going to be no speech. From a distance we watched, and what the media and others describe as an insurrection was more like a pep-rally. Aside from a few front-line agitators and some people who got tricked into pushing closer to the police lines, there was a sea of people waving flags, chanting, singing the national anthem, and pledging allegiance to the flag.

It struck me as odd that the police line fell back, repeatedly. It was like watching wrestling on television. I have seen cops working in the thick of some nasty protests and they have held the line – outnumbered and still able to control whatever aggressive crowd there was. Even though 99.99% of people in that area were not advancing, the police kept falling back until the space was filled by the growing crowd, they drew in closer to the Capitol, with some eventually going inside. After the word spread through the crowd that a protester named Ashli Babbitt had been shot and killed inside, I had seen enough. Everything about that day felt like a setup. Two years later at the time of writing this, that is an obvious fact. Many innocent and non-violent protestors who went into the building that day and walked around are still being held as political prisoners.

As we were grabbing hot dogs from the food trucks almost 3 hours from when we first approached the Capitol area, the first police cars were pulling up. I would love to hear an answer as to why it took that long for reinforcements to arrive if it was such a serious threat. It was an excellent choice not to go any further than we did that day. Whatever we thought was going to happen that day did not, and I was not interested in sticking around for the rest of the mess.

THE F.B.I

A year and three weeks after the January 6th rally, my phone rang one evening while I was at the gym. The number calling was a Washington D.C. number. A detailed message was left by an FBI agent from the local field office in Cherry Hill, New Jersey. It was an attempt to lure me in to answer some questions. The FBI had called the man in charge of my security detail that day to question him on the matter as well.

At the time, I had just begun to explore my options for Congressional run, and it seemed odd they waited to call until after rumors were circulating that I was running. I connected with a highly recommended attorney. We sat down and discussed where I was on January 5th and 6th, every anti-government tweet I have ever posted, every word I have said in speeches, and anything that could be twisted and used against me. We mapped out every possible angle the FBI had for calling me, and all the options to protect myself from this witch-hunt.

The attorney and I made a deal. I paid him a hefty fee upfront with the understanding that this fee would either be the most expensive "get lost" phone call I would ever pay someone to make or the least expensive trial bill anyone would ever pay. Thankfully, it turned out to be the most expensive phone call I have ever bought. The attorney let the FBI know that unless they had formal charges to bring against me, there would be no cooperation or answering of questions.

IF IT WAS NOT AN INSURRECTION, WHAT WAS IT?

Having been a witness of what really happened on January 6th, it breaks my heart to know that so many people have been locked up and had their lives turned upside down as part of a political agenda. Everyone who was there that day would agree – except for the agitators and infiltrators – this was no violent insurrection.

It was hard to deny the support that Trump had throughout the country, no matter what the people counting the ballots said. The number of people showing up at election fraud rallies around the country and in DC was staggering. The people who came to DC on January 6th love this country and represent the diverse and unified American spirit. One of the things I am most grateful for in the years since the start of the lockdowns, is that they brought people of every background together as patriots.

The Capitol building was a trap laid by some powerful interests in Washington. It was made possible by just a few bad actors in a crowd of well over a million people. A few people dressed in MAGA hats yelling that we needed to take the capitol, a few bad cops who opened doors for people to come in, some well-placed photographers conveniently waiting inside the Capitol, and a few media outlets and talking heads on Twitter that were ready to run with the story of an insurrection.

The resulting witch hunt after that day has turned regular Americans – many of whom have never been in any trouble – into convicted felons and has burdened them with stressful and financially destructive legal battles. The size and frequency of large protests – especially regarding the election – was proving to be problematic for the uniparty that runs Washington. Regardless of how you feel about Trump, he ignited a populist movement that presented itself as a danger to politics as usual in DC.

Since that day, there has not been one large protest a anything in the country. That is not because people have ...ut wanted to protest, it is because they are terrified to.

Most Americans do not buy the insurrection story, but all you need is a quarter of the voter base to believe it and the bulk of mainstream media to lie in our faces to make the story of the insurrection work. And they do. History is being falsely written in front of our faces; it is important that we do not allow that lie to be told.

CHAPTER 9:

"A politician thinks of the next election
 - a statesman of the next generation."
 - James Freeman Clarke

WHAT IS A LEADER?

When we stood up and fought the state, I did not know what we were up against, I just knew that what was happening to Americans was wrong. It was not until reopening did the true meaning of our fight become clear. This was not a shutdown; it was a hostile takeover of our country. Fourteen days was a bait and switch for the biggest wealth and power grab this country has ever seen.

From the moment our story broke, messages began to pour in from people looking for help, advice, and direction –

thousands of them. First, the messages were about lockdowns and opening businesses, then defunding the police, vaccine mandates, others being fined and punished, not being able to get medical treatment, and so much more. I did my best to respond to as many people as possible, even if it was just an acknowledgment of someone else's struggles and resistance.

At the gym, in public, airports, at speaking engagements and almost everywhere else I went, I was approached by people thanking me for being a leader, wanting to take a picture, and giving hugs and handshakes. I did not know what it meant to be a leader, but I would learn. Each time I was able to help someone by being honest, supportive, and inspiring, I found my new position more natural.

During the first year of reopening, supporters would often chant or hold up signs saying "Ian for Governor" at speaking engagements. This started as a joke, but I remember the calls becoming more serious as time passed and the state waged its war against the gym. The Governor's race runs off cycle in New Jersey and we had an election in 2021. Even had I wanted to, the battle was at its peak and there was no time for anything other than keeping the gym open. With no experience or idea where to start, I would not have been able to just spontaneously launch such a massive campaign.

ON THE BACK END.

It was 21 months before we had the municipal court hearing where we were finally allowed to speak to a judge in person. Nothing had been resolved yet, but I was confident we were on the back end. The constant battle with the state had begun to slow to a crawl and no new lockdowns or punishments were coming our way. Based on the way the judge treated us that day, it was clear that we would have our day in court and had survived the worst of the storm. That proved to be true.

I was proud of what we did. We had played a great defensive game against the government. They brought everything they had to crush our business and we repelled them every time. Once the township surrendered our business license, the rest began to fall apart for the state.

As that was slowly happening, I asked myself what would be next. It feels like as Americans we are always running to the fight, always rushing to put out a fire, always reacting to bad government. It comes from the right; it comes from the left. Establishment politics on either side have not served the American people for a long time. There is always a crisis that the government uses to push their way further into our lives and somehow things just keep getting worse - more taxes, debt, and regulation in exchange for fewer liberties, opportunities, and independence. Watching how all politicians sat around and got paid during COVID while they pretended to fight back as Americans suffered physically, mentally, and financially during all of it was enough for me to not trust most of them.

I thought to myself, "Where was my congressman during this? Why did not we see any involvement from the GOP while businesses were being crushed?" They tweeted about lockdowns but never stepped foot in our gym or any other small business in New Jersey that stood against restrictions. I did not want to sit around and wait for the next thing to happen. If we continue to leave politics to career politicians, we will continue to have politics as usual.

I realized I did not know who my congressman was. It was not due to a lack of interest in politics, it was because he – like many – does not do much in his district. He drops in for the occasional photo-op and campaigning activities when he needs to be reelected. His name is Andy Kim, and he represents Phil Murphy and the establishment-left that had terrorized small businesses here in New Jersey.

How were we ever going to solve the real problems that Americans face when we allow the same type of selfish, greedy, immoral people to walk into the halls of power unchallenged? If we do not dismantle the idea of the career politician and bring back the idea of elected officials being public servants, we will always be running to the fight, putting out the fires, and playing defense off our back foot.

I decided that I would run for congress. We need more of "us" to run and challenge the unchecked political ruling class. I knew that if I threw my hat in the ring, which would put me right back in the sights of everyone who hates me. I kept those thoughts to myself while I thought through my options. I started thinking about the reasons why I should not run. There were plenty of reasons for me not to do this. The story of the gym was slowly coming to a close and I was enjoying a more laid back life, if I ran, my privacy would be gone, I would be targeted, ridiculed, lied about, and judged by strangers, my personal goals would have to wait, it would be tough on my family, and I would be sacrificing all my time to a race in a challenging district. The problem is that good, regular people are discouraged from running for all of these reasons and we leave the job to people that serve their own interests first. The game of politics is intentionally dirty to keep the people that should be in it out. I knew if I did not at least try, that I would deeply regret sitting on the sidelines. This was going to radically change my life, again.

My decision to run came when I saw who was running as a republican against unseat Andy Kim - Bob Healey. I looked at this man and saw another soft, vanilla republican who represents the uniparty of DC politics – establishment republicans are the professional losers of the political game, always coming up short. These are the same republicans who sat around and watched American businesses and civil liberties get crushed under the weight of COVID mandates. I knew the problem with politics was that we always get to pick between the lesser of two evils, settling for the "best option" instead of having good ones.

I knew the chances of me winning were slim. Not only was I running in a +10-democrat district, but I was also a political outsider to the establishment GOP. I would have few allies within the system, if any. Win or lose, I wanted to make them uncomfortable, inspire other Americans to run for office, bring light to the dark and dirty world of politics, and to be a voice of common sense for the average American.

NOW WHAT?

After deciding to run, I had to figure out how to launch a campaign. The people I told were excited to hear about it and everyone wanted to help – I got referral after referral for people to contact. After meeting with half a dozen consultants, I was not impressed by the schmoozing or the posturing. I remember being at a dinner with the head of one consulting company and he flashed his vaccine passport after asking me to have a drink in NYC after the event. He clearly did not know his audience.

I turned to Chris Konawel, who was a supporter of the gym early on and someone who ran for local office and won on his second attempt as a county commissioner. He allowed me to pick his thoughts and learn a lot about the complicated process of running a campaign. He suggested I meet with a political strategist named Steve Kush, who ran Konawel's campaign and was responsible for helping Edward Durr – the New Jersey truck driver – defeat state senator and career politician Steve Sweeney, who led the state's legislative chamber for 12 years and had been suggesting hints of a 2025 run for governor. Durr's campaign was a grassroots movement that spent a fraction of what Sweeney spent and energized the same base of people who had supported the gym. I was intrigued that Kush was able to achieve so much with so little, against a political giant like Sweeney.

Kush came to the gym to meet with me and my partner, and a second time with my family. I wanted to make sure everyone understood what running for office would look like, because just like reopening the gym, I would need help from a lot of people, and I would be completely consumed by it. There were a million questions, but I was impressed with his ability to explain it all in simple terms. We discussed how we would keep it a grassroots movement, that we would stick with who I was, some goals I had for the campaign, and all the possible obstacles we would have to overcome. I was warned repeatedly that it would get ugly, that they would throw my past in my face as hard as they could, and they would be relentless. Politics is a dirty game, Kush warned me.

A CRASH COURSE IN CAMPAIGNING.

Kush gave me a crash course on running for office - what would be expected of me, what to expect of others, and what the timeline looked like. There was an enormous amount of work to be done in a short time. Running a congressional campaign is a massive undertaking that requires a strategy, contingency plans, PR, fundraising, canvassing, events, and more. To navigate the swampy waters, you need to build a team of consultants who handle dozens of tasks at any given moment. True to our mission to stay grassroots, we built out a barebones team of four consultants and a bunch of volunteers. Most consultants are opportunistic, profit driven, deeply entangled in the "politics" of politics, and are recycled through candidate after candidate. This is a major problem most Americans have very little knowledge of and something I wanted to avoid. I trusted Kush to build out an honest, small, scrappy, and efficient team – he did. We tapped into the massive network of local supporters throughout New Jersey and Pennsylvania to offer their time volunteering. The paperwork was filed, and it was official, "Ian Smith for Congress" was happening.

To run a successful campaign, you need two things: people and money. People help generate money and money helps reach more people. The political world is dominated by big money interests, which makes it difficult for the average person to generate any serious momentum with a campaign. Without name recognition or a big sum of money to start with, it is hard to be seen, heard, or taken seriously. It is no wonder we do not see regular Americans in politics, the entry price is extremely high. Those same big money interests select the bulk of our politicians, and this was something I hoped to change - or at least help expose.

Your first big task is an announcement, with an aim to generate excitement and support for your campaign. Once the foundational tasks were completed, I selected the place to make my formal announcement. I chose the VFW near my home. The purpose of the campaign was to serve the people and I thought that making my announcement at a place dedicated to people who have already served their community was a good fit. The announcement was made public for all to attend on social media, in the press, and through as many channels as we could push it through.

THE ANNOUNCEMENT.

True to our grassroots promise, the event was staged by friends, family, volunteers, and me. This was not suit and tie, country club politics, nor did I want it to be. I walked into my own announcement with a twenty-pound bag of ice slung over my shoulder for the refreshments and was greeted by many of the familiar faces who supported me over the last two years.

Part of me was wondering if anyone was going to show up but as the VFW filled up, I found myself once again standing shoulder to shoulder with people who love me.

Standing in front of the cameras and the crowd packed into the small VFW, I got nervous again for the first time since my original appearance on Tucker Carlson in 2020. I was reading my speech, which I had never done before. I was always telling the story of the gym and speaking from the heart. For this speech, I needed to make sure I hit certain points and I knew the media would be ready to pick apart what I said - every word counts. It was awkward because it immediately made me feel like a politician. I spoke to the crowd about the issues we faced as Americans - just as I had many times before - but this time it was different, we were bringing the fight to Washington D.C. I hated my speech, and I would not read a speech for the rest of my campaign. I went back to speaking from the heart at all of my engagements. Even if the message was not perfectly delivered to touch on all my political talking points, I was speaking honestly and I wanted to connect my district – republican, democrat, and independent.

Less than twenty minutes after I made my formal announcement of my intention to run for Congress, the sitting Congressman Andy Kim sent out an email blast to his supporters warning them about my campaign and advising all his supporters that they needed to fundraise more on top of their $3 million campaign fund. At the same time, my opponent in the primary election, Bob Healey, sent out a press release that was almost identical to Andy Kim's fundraising email. The DNC and the GOP had the same talking points, no surprise there. Our campaign was already disrupting the status quo and making both sides nervous.

The response was overwhelmingly positive from members at the gym, locals in District 3 and the rest of New Jersey, and people around the country. The negativity was expected, and it came just as it had come many times before. There were always some people who suddenly had a problem with what I was doing. The same criticisms and insults were thrown at me and my family. I have been asked about this frequently through the last three years – how to handle criticism from strangers, what to do when you lose friends due to differences of opinion, jealousy, and whatever else. My friend - author Jack Donovan - summed this up perfectly in his book "Becoming a Barbarian." There is a chapter in it called "No Apologies, No Arguments, No Explanations" and in it he beautifully lays out why you should not worry about these three things with people who are not important to you. Apologies are for those you love, because you hurt them. Arguments are for your friends and family, because you want them to understand you. Explanations are for those you respect, because you value their approval. As Jack says, "No one respects a man who is always apologizing and backpedaling. No one respects a man who is always asking for permission. No one respects a man who will not stand up for himself or fight for his own interests." I read that during my time at the gym and it stuck with me through the intense criticism and losses because of my actions. Growth scares people and it makes them uncomfortable, and the way they deal with their fear is to try to hold you back or bring you down. Your journey will not wait for you while you worry about the opinions of people who do not wish you well - old friends included.

THE DAILY GRIND.

Campaigning is exciting, it offers new challenges every day. You get to meet and collaborate with amazing people, and there is always somewhere to be and something to do. It is also exhausting, there are a lot of boring tasks to do. Once the campaign kicked off, I had four major tasks to handle until the election: fundraising, events and media, endorsements, and canvassing the district talking to voters.

Fundraising sucks. Unless you are a party-approved candidate with personal wealth and/or connections to big donors, you are going to be grinding for every dollar. For regular candidates who are running without the support of the GOP or DNC, which means asking for small donations. I was fortunate that I had a little bit of a head start because so many people had encouraged me to run, and I had name recognition to potentially attract some bigger donors. Even with that advantage, it is an uphill battle trying to fundraise against the political machine. I utilized my social media presence to be active in discussions online, where I could reach potential voters and supporters directly by participating in conversations about current political issues. The standard method is to 'hit the phones' and cold call donors. Kush stressed the importance of raising money, so I sucked it up and did those too. In the political world, not only is the money going to run the campaign, but it also shows people that you are a candidate they can get behind. The ability to raise money is one of the standards by which candidates are measured by donors of all sizes, media, organizers, political allies, PACs, and other organizations. I got on the phone and started calling. It was uncomfortable at first, but I got the hang of it and had many good conversations with interesting people from all over the state and the country.

It was an opportunity for me to get a read on the issues that voters really cared about. Many of those calls were to older Americans, it was always a great talk when I got to speak to an old war veteran or somebody's grandmother who saw what this country was and what it had become. All said we raised over $100,00 to run the campaign, but the GOP-backed candidate had over a million dollars. Much of our fundraising came from small donors who just wanted to see someone who was more like them than the same guy that has been making empty promises for years. I took pride in knowing I did not appeal to the political machine, although this put us at a huge disadvantage. This is the reality of regular people fighting the machine – it is possible, but it was far more difficult than I had ever anticipated.

Events and media are the easy part, if you believe in what you are doing, and your heart is in the right place. Being in front of the camera and out in the district talking to voters is important to gain momentum for the campaign, and this is somewhere I excelled. Most people are not actively tuned into the primary season of politics, so getting as much media coverage on your campaign, stances, and plans to fix the issues is an important part of reaching the reliable voters. Because of our limited budget, we did not have much allocated for large advertising campaigns like text messages, TV/Radio ads, and mailers. I said yes to every journalist, blogger, podcaster, and host that would contact me, and many did. The sensationalism that surrounded the story of the gym, so we used that to leverage interest in the campaign.

We held and attended dozens of events. These events are designed more for the engaged voter; these people are more active in the primary elections, pay close attention to politics, and direct the opinions of less engaged voters. The counties and towns of the district host events for candidates, others are organized by activist groups in the area, or people hosting you in their home for a small community gathering. I went to everything I could fit into my calendar. I enjoyed this part of campaigning the most. I saw what the power of people coming together could do at the gym and it was exciting to see it in my quiet district of NJ-03. This is also where I excelled so much that my opponent started canceling public appearances where we would both be present. The stark contrast between the two of us was apparent when it came to talking off script to voters.

I wanted to make sure I gave people the chance to ask any question they wanted and feel comfortable expressing the issues that were most important to them. I was asked about policies and plans, my prison history, how I was going to be different from usual, what I would do under pressure to fall in line with the establishment, and more. Many appreciated my openness and casual approach to the campaign, but there were plenty who did not. I was booed at several events for refusing to show support for American taxpayer money being sent to support Ukraine. There was rarely a night that we did not stop at least one event to talk to voters. This kept us connected to an energized base of voters that made the GOP nervous.

When you are a small, organic campaign most of your firepower is going to come from your volunteers. It takes money to do anything, and we only had so much of it. We saved money by doing a lot of walking and canvassing the towns within the district. This was once customary practice, but today most campaigns rely heavily on paid advertisements sent directly to people's homes, phones, emails, radios, and televisions. We had about twenty consistent volunteers helping us stuff envelopes and campaign door to door with us by dropping off literature about the campaigns platform and what we wanted to accomplish. We also gave out lawn signs by the hundreds to anyone who wanted them, and dispensed teams of volunteers to put them out on major roads. I walked the district daily, picking a township and dedicating a few days to make sure I knocked on all the doors. I spent up until well after sundown doing this at least three days a week. There were many people who told me it was the first time a politician had knocked on their door in 20 years.

One woman, in a quiet corner of the district, told me she had never seen a congressional candidate come to her town - she was seventy-eight and lived there her entire life. These were some of the best conversations I had on the campaign. I made it a point to knock on the door of someone who had my opponents sign on their lawn, to have a conversation about why they liked him better or what they did not agree with in terms of my policies. Out on the roads, people would wave and honk, and get out of their cars to come grab a picture and lawn sign as I was planting them down on the highways and major intersections.

Endorsements are a powerful form of currency in politics, they can come from individuals and organizations. Certain endorsements will open the door to massive amounts of support, fundraising, and function as a stamp of approval for people unfamiliar with your campaign. Our campaign received endorsements from Kari Lake, General Michael Flynn, BlackPac, Veteran's for Trump, and many others.

During the campaign, I was invited to a private event hosted at Mar A Lago, with President Trump as the keynote speaker. After he left the stage, one of his executives invited me to join a private group dinner upstairs. I was able to sit down in the dining room with many other high profile conservative figures, candidates, and elected officials. As I sat eating my steak and joining the conversation at my table, the President walked into the dining room and was bombarded with excitement from his guest. I was so focused on scarfing the Delmonico on my plate, I did not originally notice he had walked in. He immediately spotted me and said, "New Jersey gym owner! Man, you gave them hell". I took the opportunity to get up, shake his hand, introduce myself. I let him know that I was running for congress in New Jersey and asked him for a moment of his time. He happily agreed and we spoke in private for a few minutes about New Jersey and my race. He asked me who I was running against in the Republican party, how the campaign was going, and had a lot of questions about the state of the GOP in New Jersey.

We took a couple of photos together and talked about him endorsing my race. I swung for the fences by asking him, on the spot, but I was not going to pass up the opportunity. Trump got thousands of requests for endorsements in 2022. There were people screaming during his speech earlier asking for endorsements, at least I had gotten a better ask than they did. Unfortunately, Trump did not endorse any races in all of New Jersey.

Having been recognized for what we did during the pandemic by the President and getting the opportunity to talk to him candidly was a powerful experience. Ask me three years ago - or fifteen years ago when I was in prison - if I ever could have imagined I would find myself in that position. I would have laughed at the question. All because I opened my gym.

WINS AND LOSSES.

Ultimately, I lost the primary election to the GOP favorite in a three-way race. Bob Healey took a little more than half of the vote, with about 40% for me, and the remainder to the third candidate. To say I was disappointed would be an understatement. We had more energy, authenticity, and support for our campaign but were unable to beat back the textbook play of the establishment to "go negative" and hammer voters with negative ads about me. I was an easy target and they had plenty of money to spend. It worked beautifully for them.

Despite the loss, we achieved a lot. I have met dozens of people throughout the country who ran at the same time as me for local positions and won. They cited the inspiration they got from seeing my race as one of the reasons they stepped up to serve on the school board or in their municipal and county government. There are even more running this election cycle. Our campaign energized a base of voters who felt left behind by typical GOP politicians and made the establishment spend a lot of money to beat us. It felt good watching these people sweat when their plans got disrupted. This needs to happen in every district and every position in this country, and it could, very easily.

Part of the problem we face as Americans is that we do not challenge these systems enough. Most of us – me included – do not pay attention during the primary election and therefore allow our candidates to be selected for us. Typically, the GOP and DNC hand-picked candidates walk through the primaries with little opposition. Imagine if people organized challenges to them in every office. Sure, we would not win them all, but we would win some. If there are seven people on your school board and only one "good once" gets elected, you now have a foothold. Next year, if two more get in, you almost have a majority. In three years, the tides could turn. This is being done quite well in some places, but we need to see more of it throughout the country. Collectively, we need to start thinking about and executing on this. Do it repeatedly, starting with local politics. I walked away from the campaign with the clear understanding that local and state politics need to be obtained and secured before the American people regain control over the out of control politics of Washington D.C. Regular Americans have a chance at the local level to get elected and then can make much more of an impact there than they can being vastly outnumbered on Capitol Hill.

I was disappointed in the low voter turnout. Even at a time when people were clearly upset about the direction the country is heading, only about 20% of registered voters participated. For months after the election, I had people approaching me telling me they could not wait to vote for me, completely unaware that they had missed the opportunity to do so. Thomas Jefferson spoke on the importance of having a well-informed population to protect what they had built. The Founding Fathers knew that our republic could lead to tyranny. Representative democracy opens the possibility of selfish people getting elected. This happens when the public is less informed, less educated, and less involved in public service. The "Let somebody else do it" mindset. We need to learn collectively to be more engaged in our political process. Showing up at the polls for the general election once every 2 years or so is not an acceptable contribution to your community or country. If that is all someone is willing to do to protect their freedoms, then they do not deserve to be free.

In the end, my loss was ultimately my fault. I did not give the campaign enough time to plan and fully execute – that was because of me. I waited until the final hour to do something I knew I should do. I wasted time going back and forth in my own head, debating back and forth about if I should run. I let the fear of the opinions and criticisms of strangers slow me down. I underestimated the power of party politics, and I thought it would be easier. I was overconfident from beating back the New Jersey government when they tried to close my gym down. That overconfidence led me to delay my decision, as if I did not need every second leading up to the election to run against the establishment. My team did their best with what I gave them, and, in the end, I did not give them enough.

The biggest mistake, however, was not listening to Kush. At the onset of the campaign, he and I sat down, and I had to tell him every bad thing about me: my darkest secrets, most embarrassing moments, every law I have ever broken, every vice I have ever had, and anything else I could possibly come up with that might be used against me. He warned me, very clearly, that I was an easy target for them to run negative attacks on. He said that they would actively look for new ways to claim that I was unfit for the office. He told me never to go anywhere completely alone, so I always had somebody to vouch for me. He told me that no matter what the occasion was, to not have a single drink in public. I broke that rule one evening when I had a drink at a friend's birthday dinner. Later that evening, I was pulled over on the way home. I was honest about that with the officer about having a drink. He asked me to do a sobriety test, I performed well and was immediately arrested anyway.

Regardless of whether it was true or not, I gave my opponents a golden ticket. The same journalists that called me a dangerous ex-felon for reopening the gym jumped at the opportunity to call me a dangerous drunk. Both Andy Kim and Bob Healey piled on - why wouldn't they? I immediately called for the police to release the video of the stop, so that people could see what happened and form their own opinions – it was seen by millions. I made my public statement on it and was thoroughly embarrassed as I was criticized, questioned, and ridiculed by haters and supporters alike. I deserved it. Plenty of people aggressively rushed to my defense after seeing the footage. Either way, I should not have put any of them in the position to have to do that. This was a hard pill to swallow because no matter how innocent I knew I was, I looked like a real fucking idiot. I could only be mad at myself though; Kush expressly warned me for this specific reason.

If the election was a race around the track, this was the part where we were way ahead, and I fell flat on my face. I got back up and our campaign regained a lot of the lost support as more information came out and I answered questions about it publicly. However, we did not have enough time left to regain what was needed for me to secure the win.

The DUI charge was dropped after the primary election in October of 2022. Big surprise there. It was nice to finally be vindicated, but the damage had been done. It is not fun being drug through the mud, but it will make you tougher. You realize that you do not have to give value to every opinion about you. You realize that not everyone is your friend, but your devoted friends will be the ones who show up when you need them most. You also realize that you should listen to those friends when they try to give you advice. It was a hard lesson to learn, but it humbled me, and I think I needed that.

I am proud of the campaign we ran. I am grateful for every volunteer who donated their time to the campaign. I value all the input I received from the families I met going door-to-door. I will always cherish the fact that people opened their homes to our campaign, invited me to speak at their events, walk the Memorial Day parade with them, and the trust that was put in me with the casting of their ballot. Though disappointed I lost, I was also glad to be out of the mucky waters of politics. I walked away with the understanding that the change we need is not just a political one, but more importantly a cultural one. What matters most is not who we vote for, or what side we think we are on, but how we contribute to our communities by being engaged in productive efforts. How engaged we are. When we hosted Veterans Outreach at the gym and I got to help with many other events around the country, I saw that bringing people together solves problems in our community. It unites us behind issues we can all get behind. Imagine if we all picked a few good things to sacrifice our time, energy, and money to each year; what impact would that have on our communities and our country? I am not suggesting anyone stop paying attention to or participating in politics. Just a better distribution of our attention to where it can serve us best. We have more power and influence than we think we do as individuals – everything we do matters.

CHAPTER 10:

RULES FOR REBELLION

"Rebellion against tyrants
is obedience to God."
- Benjamin Franklin

MEDIA MATTERS.

From the beginning, I knew that media coverage and social awareness was going to be an essential element of our survival and ability to fight back. All the punishment endured would be worth it if we could show the people of the country just how far politicians would go to ensure our compliance with their orders. Take punches, keep a cool head, and show everyone the truth by continuing to open the gym no matter how the state would try to punish us.

Going against the system is scary because you are playing their game, and they are both player and referee. That is just the way it is, resistance to tyranny will always come with unfair treatment. What made that fear manageable is being able to broadcast it and show the world what was happening to our business, and thousands of others. Through a series of fortunate events starting with the decision to send our public statement into the Rich Zeoli show, I was able to build out our own broadcast system across social media, TV, radio, newspapers, documentaries, and public speaking. Because our movement was organic, it was hard to contain. People took an interest in the story, shared it, talked about it, called into the radio about it, and genuinely followed it. At the height of the chaos, I would consistently post updates about the gym, and they would easily average twenty thousand reshares and hundreds of thousands of likes, comments, and views. Because people cared so much, the news would pick up the story time after time and because it was on the news so frequently people stayed informed about what was going on – one fed the other. Even as the news cycle swallowed other stories whole, the media kept covering the defiant New Jersey gym owners.

IF YOU WANT HELP, HELP OTHERS.

Throughout the lockdown and mandates, I traveled the country going to events. Organizers called regularly, looking to get me to come speak at their events, or to share the event information with our supporters. I spent a lot of time fighting my way through airports, and driving long distances through the night, but I was able to use my voice to help others. The more I put into helping others, the more others helped the gym. If we had only focused on our problems at the gym, our support would have dwindled long before the fight was over.

THICK SKIN.

In the age of the internet, everyone has an opinion and anonymity allows people to get nasty without fear of repercussions.

Most people are terrified of being criticized. I know I was. It came hard and fast for me and all of us at the gym. The first big wave came with our announcement video and my appearance on Tucker Carlson. As soon as the segment was over, we received hundreds of threatening phone calls and a barrage of comments online calling us grandma killers, selfish, and threats to society. It is overwhelming when thousands of people are attacking you through every communication channel. The fear of that alone is enough to keep most people quiet and unwilling to stand for what is right.

One of the most common criticisms we got was that we - and all who came to our gym - were selfish because we only cared about muscles. Anyone saying that has clearly never been to the gym. Mental health is always the underlying reason behind the physical actions of the gym. What gave us the strength to endure the nasty criticisms was hearing how thankful our members were for being able to do what makes them happy, feel good, be less stressed, control their anxiety or PTSD, and all the other reasons.

When the journalists came after me about my fatal automobile accident almost 15 years prior, I wanted to crawl into a hole and quit. The sad part is many of them got the details wrong, exposing the fact that they did not actually care, they just wanted to use it against me to intimidate me into stopping what we were doing. The stories went national, and I received thousands of threatening phone calls, death threats, and never-ending criticism from cowards online over the course of the two years keeping the gym open. I chose to address the criticisms directly and continue my course. What we were doing was too important and the critics wanted me to quit, I knew that.

There were wild accusations online about how I was a racist, and then a sexist, and whatever the next 'ist' would be. Family and friends were criticized and threatened for associating with me. There were plenty of longtime friends, clients, and family members that turned their backs – never to be heard from again. I had to learn to accept that for what it was. However, the friends and family who stuck around and the new ones who became a part of my circle outweigh any losses. Through it all, the people that are a part of life today are more valuable to me than anything I sacrificed.

There is an odd freedom in putting yourself up for punishment. Once the beating begins, you realize there is little reason for you to be afraid. Words do not hurt as much as most of us fear they will.

GET COMFORTABLE BE-ING UNCOMFORTABLE.

Picking a fight with the government, or any powerful entity, does not come without its fair share of sacrifice. That is how the game works, and that is how success works in any regard. Going against the state just makes it more interesting, because you are going head-to-head with people that have no morals and unlimited funding.

There is a quote by Voltaire from The Age of Louis XIV, "It is dangerous to be right in matters on which the established authorities are wrong." Though an obvious statement, it is not one that many Americans considered thoroughly before the COVID lockdowns. Many were blissfully ignorant of the looming threat of big government before March of 2022 – enjoying the comforts of living in a place like America. I certainly was. I was not even paying attention to politics at the time, aside from enjoying the feel-good Nationalism and economy under President Trump.

It needs to be understood that in matters of personal freedom, there is always a price you pay to either establish, defend, or protect that freedom. That price you pay is often in the form of being unfairly punished or sacrificing valuable assets like your time, money, property, and even your life. Freedom is precious because it is paid for at a high price.

We tend to think of threats to freedom coming from external foes and defended with guns, but we are just as likely – if not more – to have to guard our liberties against our own government as we are a foreign one. The COVID response was a clear case of the dangers associated with giving people authority over you. When you find yourself in a situation where you must rebel, expect to be treated unfairly in your defiance.

I say this because many wanted to avoid conflict and were hesitant to speak up and get involved during COVID because they feared the consequences – loss of a job, a friendship or relationship, a fine, an unpleasant argument at the grocery store for not wearing a mask. The reality, however, is that if you do not participate and support causes you care about – the world will always happen to you, and not because of you. We underestimate the importance of our involvement in social and political matters. If people understood how impactful they really are, they would be much more inclined to welcome the discomfort associated with standing for what they know is right.

One of the best characteristics I was able to develop is the capacity to suffer for a cause. Pick how you want to apply that – business, in the gym, financially, or anything else in life. If you can be comfortable taking hits and sacrificing something, there is not much you will not accomplish.

ADDRESSING THE ELEPHANT IN THE ROOM.

We were early adopters when it came to COVID resistance. When we reopened the gym, most people were still quiet about what they were thinking. People were trying to just ride it out. Early on, we addressed the elephant in the room - the uncomfortable truth. None of this made sense and when we tried to make sense of it, the only conclusion we could arrive at is that politicians were screwing us all over. For us, it was liberating coming to terms with the worst-case scenario. If we allowed the government to shut us down for any longer than we had, it would have been a slow death until we were no longer able to sustain the losses. That was clear and there was no denying it. We had to be brutally honest with ourselves – these people were going to destroy us.

That was the worst case, therefore nothing the state could do to us was worse. We were free.

Arrest us? Not as bad as losing the business we built.

Fine us? Not as bad as losing the business we built.

Prison? Not as bad as losing the business we built.

This is hard to come to terms with, but once you do, you can act confidently with a clear head and be unmovable in your convictions.

EVERYBODY TAKES THEIR HITS.

Through all my encounters, I have seen and heard brave stories of sacrifice from people all over the country. The cause was the same, the vessel was often different. We opened a gym, others quit their jobs, went to prison, were kicked out of the military, and more. The sacrifices of individuals are often overlooked amidst bigger news stories, but they are no less significant in their impact.

Early in the lockdowns, my friend Greg Anderson willingly lost his job as a police officer after explicitly stating in a video that he would not enforce unconstitutional mandates. His words went viral, and it was not received well by his commanding officers. Greg is a father and a provider. He took his stand at a time when almost no other police officer had and was the first man through the door. Citizens had not started getting upset with cops this early on. He could have stayed quiet, just let people off and kept his head low. He chose the harder path because it was what was right.

I met a young Marine while speaking in Anaheim, he told me that he was refusing the vaccine mandate and all troubles it had caused him. He said to me that our actions had inspired him to make his choice – he was one of five on his base who would not comply. These young Marines were being dragged through the mud with unfair treatment, reprimanded with otherwise outstanding records, and threatened to be discharged for their refusal to comply. When someone you have never met tells you something of that magnitude, it is lifechanging. Never again would I doubt the power of individual actions.

Both are fine today. Life has a way of working out for the best when you do the right thing – even if you go through challenges getting there. None of it is easy, but it is worth doing. If you would ask either of those men if they regret what they did, they will say no. Even those like Danny Presti, the owner of Mac's Public House, who fought NYC and had to close his business, would say they do not regret their decision.

COVID lockdowns forced a lot of us to make hard choices and sacrifices, but there is a lesson in there. If we understand that discomfort and sacrifice are the price of freedom, then we can be more prepared to make those tough choices when they come. When Ben Franklin said, "A republic, if you can keep it." He was referring to the sacrifices of time, money, energy, and punishment to keep a society free, strong, and together. The people who came before us understood that freedom will always be tested, and we must be vigilant in our efforts to protect it.

CRITICAL MASS.

The path to change is always a long series of cause and effect. One person's actions impact the next person's, which leads to an exponential increase in the number of people involved. What started as a couple hundred people in the gym parking lot turned into an army of supporters. The game ends when enough people are inspired to stand up, meet resistance, and stay standing, until they run out of ways to enforce their tyrannical orders. In America, if we had not hit a critical mass of non-compliance, we would all be living under the same type of COVID policies that the Chinese have submitted to.

EMBRACE THE SUCK.

If we know that we are going to be treated unfairly for standing up for ourselves, it is critical that we learn to have some while we are in the thick of it. At the gym, we had fun every day, even on the days when we got pummeled with bad news. If it is always serious, eventually you will burn out. We laughed and joked, made light of everything we could, and we set out to make the whole thing look as absurd as it was.

When companies started giving away free stuff to people who rushed to get their vaccine without knowing anything about it, we offered free memberships (we were already free) to anyone who did not get vaccinated. When they came to lock our doors, we took them off. When they said no holidays with family, we held a New Year's Eve party at the gym. When the government took our money, we made T-shirts making fun of the Governor.

My adventures with the TSA during COVID are a prime example. We all experienced the battle of going to a store without a mask on or trying to eat without a vaccine card. Flying without a mask was even more of a clown show. As I traveled the country to speak and raise money for the gym's legal battles, I needed to fly dozens of times. Because I had taken a definitive and public stance on mask policy at the gym – even getting fined $15k daily for not enforcing it – there was no way I could be seen wearing a mask when flying. I had been one of loudest when it came to mandatory masking and our refusal to comply at the gym was well known. I could not put one on to get on a plane just because it was more convenient at the moment. Once I made that stand, there was no going back.

The first few flights were easy, it was more like a game of cat-and-mouse. Entering the airport, you were bombarded with employees telling you to pull your mask up, put it on, and follow the arrows on the floors. My strategy was to keep moving and have something in my hand to drink – we all tried this move at least once. It worked in the airport, but trying to get through TSA without a mask on was like trying to get into Fort Knox. With nothing to hold in your hands, this was the point where you had to put on a mask, and they were adamant about it. I would grab a mask and act like a clueless passenger, get lost in the masses, and when questioned about where my mask was, I would point back to another agent saying that they had told me to go ahead through. Most people enforcing masks were as annoyed by having to enforce it as everyone was having to wear them. That worked a few times, and a few times when it did not, I had to leave the airport and get in a rental car to drive 12 or more hours to my destination. There was no way I was wearing one.

Getting through TSA maskless was the first hurdle but being on the plane was the real fight. There, you had to battle both flight attendants and psychotic passengers who were convinced you were secretly walking around with the plague – God forbid you sneezed. Following the same basic strategy by always having something to eat or drink worked once or twice, but not for long. When I flew home after speaking at CPAC 2021 on American Airlines, I was told numerous times to put my mask on. I politely refused and continued to eat one peanut at a time out of my endless supply. Upon arrival back in Philadelphia, there were Air Marshalls and police waiting for me. I was scolded like a child for my dangerous behavior. I asked if I was under arrest, but nobody had anything to say, so I walked away and went home. A day later, I had an email from American Airlines notifying me that I was banned from flying until further notice. As I continued my defiance, other airlines followed this action. Weeks later, on a Delta flight, I was removed from the plane by threat of force and imprisonment for not complying with mask mandates. Within months, I was restricted to flying the only three remaining airlines that had not banned me – United, Frontier, and Spirit.

After the Delta incident, the TSA decided that I was a security threat because of my behavior and that any further issues would result in me being put on a no-fly list. They sent me a threatening letter, scolding me for my defiant behavior abord the flights. I had upset enough people along the way by refusing to wear a mask. I ignored the letter and booked my next flight for the next speaking engagement. At this point, I had found a doctor who was not going along with the COVID hysteria, and he wrote me a mask exemption.

If you ever want to feel like a criminal, just piss off the TSA. The next time I flew I was unable to check in on my phone and received instructions to show up early at the airport and go to the ticket counter. After the airline employee pulled up my name, several managers and employees came over and began to point at the screen and then picked up the phone to resolve the issue. I was now officially on the TSA's naughty list, better known as SSSS: Secondary Security Screening Selection. After a 30-minute phone call, the TSA cleared the airline to print my ticket and TSA officers came to escort me to my own lane at the TSA checkpoint to experience the VIP treatment. The process took an hour and a half, often much longer. First, you go through the metal detector, then get wanded, then you go through the X-ray machine, and finish that off with a full body pat – checking even the seams of your clothing, your hands from explosive residue, and more. After that, they tear apart your luggage completely, every item comes out and is thoroughly searched and swabbed for explosive residue. You get to watch as they destroy your belongings and leave you to repack them. I sat and waited for another thirty minutes while a manager called in the search and reported that I was in fact not a domestic terrorist. I was free to go, but not without my TSA officer escorting me around the airport (even the bathroom) until I boarded the flight.

This became standard, I remained on the SSSS list for over a year and a half – every time I flew – until I filed multiple appeals to be taken off the list. I traveled frequently during COVID, sometimes three times a month and had to show up at the airport three or four hours early just to be harassed. I continued to fight with people over masking, being removed from flights even when I had an exemption, and more. Many would say, "just wear the mask, you are making a big deal over nothing" but I was unwilling to participate in the nonsense of pretending that masks worked. If there is no resistance to what is clearly wrong, they will continue to do wrong. You might as well make these people work for it, make their lives miserable for enforcing such lunacy. Eventually the enforcers get tired of the nonsense as well, and it starts to fall apart. If everyone complies, we go further down the path of illogical control and tyranny.

Was it a pain in the ass? Sure. Did it make my life uncomfortable and inconvenient? Sure. Will I do it again if they ever try that again? Absolutely. I learned to have fun with it instead of being upset by the inconvenience and because of that, it was not so bad. To the credit of many TSA officers and airline employees, I had a ton of funny, enjoyable moments being treated like a domestic terrorist. I flew so frequently that the entire TSA at the Philadelphia airport knew me and agents at airports throughout the country would recognize me from previous trips and media appearances. Many thanked me for the work we did and told me that they were resisting the vaccine mandate and other unconstitutional orders within their workplace.

CHAPTER 11:

MORE GAINED THAN LOST

"In the beginning of a change the
patriot is a scarce man, and brave,
and hated and scorned. When his cause
succeeds, the timid join him, for then
it costs nothing to be a patriot."
- Mark Twain

WAS IT ALL WORTH IT?

Absolutely. Shortly after the congressional campaign ended, I sold my stake at the gym to my former partner. Partnerships are tough, they require a lot of work, and if you add in the stress of fighting an entire state government it makes things much harder. After fighting so hard, this was not the outcome I wanted, but that is life sometimes. We held contrasting views and no longer agreed on the path forward for the gym. Once the business license had been reinstated, the gym was able to function like a normal business – no longer relying on donations to stay open. The municipal charges remained but our previous encounter with the judge made it clear that was not a threat. Any other court proceedings were claims against the state. The fight was over.

We had withstood the storm and made it through to the other side of the fight – so many businesses were not so fortunate in their efforts. Though I was not happy about leaving the gym behind, it was what was best for everyone involved. I love the gym, the members, and the massive community that formed around it between 2020-2022. I am proud of all we did with that community – sending the lockdown plans of the New Jersey government into a tailspin, inspiring thousands to fight back in their own ways. I am grateful for the people that made it all possible. I still see people wearing the "Bellmawr for Everybody" shirt at airports, events, online, and in gyms all over the country – a reminder of the stand we all took.

The events of the last two years had opened a world of new challenges and opportunities. The most important of which was being a new father. Shortly before I sold the gym, I learned that I had a son on the way. I had something worth fighting for before, but this changed everything. Spending my life behind the counter of gym in a hostile partnership was not what I wanted for myself and my growing family. After moving on from the gym, I launched a new business and became a partner in two more projects. I have reclaimed autonomy of my life after being stuck at the gym. The incredible network of friends around me has allowed me those opportunities. There was a time in my life where I did not know what that felt like – to have a support system that believed in me and people who were excited to collaborate with me. That kind of trust is earned through actions. There is nothing that I would trade for the circle of people around me and the lessons learned throughout the last couple of years. The Roman playwright Plautus said, "Where there are friends, there is wealth" and by that standard I am wealthy.

HOW DO WE RECLAIM OUR COUNTRY?

I have traveled the country speaking, telling the same story you just read. Sometimes part of it, sometimes the whole thing, sometimes with different details highlighted, and different lessons to be learned. Every speech shared the same purpose: to inspire others to 'Find their Hill' and get involved in the fight to preserve the freedoms and value systems that make this country great.

From a careless young man with no direction sitting in a prison cell, to running for the United States Congress while fighting the government to keep my gym open. I could have authored a book about the car accident and prison, another about the lockdowns and the gym, and one more about running for Congress. There were lessons in each of those stories, but I chose to pull them all together to connect the overarching themes that we are powerful and important beyond measure, and that we are always able to overcome great losses, tragedies, and mistakes.

The biggest lie we tell ourselves is that we are just one person, and we are too insignificant to make a difference. Ask a child what they want to be when they grow up and they will answer with a list of ambitious ideas – an astronaut, the president, a millionaire, and more. Somewhere along the line we lose that confidence to be impactful. We put our heads down and keep quiet, we do our jobs and pay our bills, and we slowly accept the big lie that we have no impact on the world around us. The gym did not stay open because we had superpowers, it stayed open because two hardheaded gym owners from a little corner of New Jersey drew their line in the sand and inspired an army of regular Americans to stand with them – at the gym and in their own lives. What makes the story particularly powerful is that it is a story about regular people. The movement was of the people, by the people, for the people – as grassroots as it gets. I would have never imagined any of this being possible just a few years ago but look at the impact we had.

We lie again and convince ourselves that our mistakes define us. Overcoming immense guilt and prison, to go on to build multiple successful businesses and run for the House of Representatives did not require any special skill set. It requires the ability to forgive yourself and a promise to be better. A comeback like that is not possible in most places in the world, but it is a fundamental characteristic of this country, of freedom.

It is important that as Americans we realize that we have something great in the culture, values, and especially freedoms in this country. We are a land of potential and possibilities for anyone willing to work for them. The expression "freedom is not free" comes from the American military observing the sacrifice of defending freedom but is a mantra for everyday American excellence as well.

There are two prices for freedom, the first is conflict and violence, the second is engaged citizenship and personal excellence. This country was built by people of all backgrounds, who fought and died for our liberties in revolution, war, and civil conflict. All we must do is preserve them is to be the best versions of ourselves. We must take advantage of the life we have been provided by becoming strong physically and mentally, educated, informed, financially responsible, industrious, compassionate, and as self-sufficient as we can be. To be free, we must develop all those characteristics, and more, by being active and engaged in our lives. When we are, we are better for our families, our families are better for our community, and our communities are better for our country.

We know that government overreach is not going away. The nonsense we witnessed during COVID is not the first, nor it is the last example of this ever-looming threat. The game of inches where they take a little, back off, and move to something else will continue until it is entirely put to bed. To preserve our freedom, we must stand vigilant against all encroachments against liberty. Long passed is the time when we can just put it all in the hands of politicians to manage while we go about our lives. This is precisely how we end up where we did in 2020 - by not paying attention and growing dependent on them for solutions.

Free countries are comprised of free people and to be free is to be strong and engaged in the choices being made around you.

Most of the time the work is not glamorous, easy, or fun, but the result is always worth the sacrifice. Those small sacrifices keep the wolves at bay. They keep children's education safe, stop the bad bills from becoming laws, get the local candidate elected, and get your family healthier – so that we never have to sacrifice in a manner that requires actual fighting. Ambitious standards for ourselves create a culture of winners, and a culture of winners are hard to oppress. When we win the small battles every day, we win the game of inches that has been played against Americans for decades. That is the way back to the country we all love, and the way forward into the future. Empowered people are free people.

Imagine if a million Americans decided to do that tomorrow. What would happen with a million more people in the gym, eating healthier, showing up at town councils and board meetings, spending and saving their money smarter, opening businesses, planting gardens, spending less time on their phones and more with their families, organizing community events and charity, and showing up during the election process? What if we scaled that million people down to your just town or your city? What would it look like if a thousand or even a hundred people in your community started doing that? What problems could we solve with that type of engaged citizenship?

This country is sick with victimhood, dependency, and apathy and the cure is excellence, autonomy, excitement. It starts with the individual. It starts with you. If you do not know where that starts or what that is, then ask yourself who or what is 'worth fighting for' – find your hill, as I call it. That looks like something different for each of us. There is not a how-to manual, and this certainly is not an attempt to write one. This is just the story of a regular guy who did his part to remind us of all how powerful we all are...

We the people...

ACKNOWLEDGEMENTS

An attempt to acknowledge all those who have impacted my life through these stories would fill another book, and still leave some out.

Thank you to everyone who believed in me, who gave me a chance, who encouraged me, who picked me up when I fell, who forgave me, and who let me lean on them when I needed it.

ABOUT THE AUTHOR

Just a regular guy who did not want to close his gym.

MORE ENDORSEMENTS

"Ian Smith is in my definition what Americans should be. Big, strong, bold, and brash. I have known Ian for some time and one thing that I will tell you is his character and integrity is second to none and will not be tarnished or broken. Ian sticks to what he believes in and that is rare these days.

He is one of the few red-blooded Americans left and I am proud to call Ian my friend and my brother."

RAY CARE (RET. NAVY SEAL)

"America loves a comeback story... Ian is that man! What I admire about him is that he learned from the burden he created for himself which landed him in prison years ago. He paid his dues and carried it to the fast lane of achievement. During COVID, when America needed someone to stand up for what was right, he led a movement that reinvigorated America's backbone to stand up against lockdowns while also helping his community... This story is a must read!"

CARL HIGBE (RET. NAVY SEAL, NEWSMAX)

"Ian is the definition of "fearless." While the world shut down businesses and common sense, Ian spoke truth to power and stood for freedom. His courage was contagious, and every Liberty-loving American can learn from his story. "

TOMI LAHREN (FOX NEWS)

"I respected Ian for risking his entire livelihood to oppose the tyrannical lockdowns. I hope in the future people will look back and use Ian as motivation to not bow down to unlawful government restrictions."

ALEX STEIN (COMEDIAN, POLITICAL ACTIVIST)

"Ian Smith is an American hero. He is not perfect, but mythic heroes never really are. Ian's just some guy who stood his ground, who pushed back against tyranny and corruption when other men wanted to but did not. In doing that, he reminded men everywhere what was possible — what we could do and should do if we want to remain free men. Smith has become a symbol of resistance and a powerful speaker, and I do not believe that this hero's journey — or his story — is over yet."

JACK DONOVAN (AUTHOR OF 'THE WAY OF MEN')

"In a world full of weaklings, one man stands out for his commitment, discipline, and courage in the face of tyranny. The trials and triumph of Ian Smith inspires and enlightens every man to grow stronger today!"

ELLIOT HULSE (MEN'S STRENGTH COACH)

"When I first met Ian, it was after someone tagged me in a post where he was wearing a LIONS NOT SHEEP hat. I was intrigued to connect with this patriot and after a simple conversation I knew he was a brother. After a tyrannical government forced him to remove the doors of his business and then watching him kick in the boards placed over those doors, I knew that there were men who would indeed stand. It takes balls to speak your mind. It takes even bigger balls to stand against oppression and say FREE MAN HERE. Ian has inspired millions of people, me included."

SEAN WHALEN (ENTREPRENEUR)

"In a world where cowardice is the norm, courage is rare, and masculinity is demonized, we are in dire need of men who stand up for their principles and the liberty of others. Ian Smith is one of them."

- ZUBY (RAPPER, AUTHOR, HOST OF THE 'REAL TALK WITH ZUBY' PODCAST)

"Ian Smith's story is truly a modern day David Vs Goliath tale that exemplifies the impact we can have when we stand our ground and fight for our God given rights.

Ian went from being the "everyman" small business and became a national hero.

In a time where fear and uncertainty was weaponized by our leaders against us, it's inspiring to see men like Ian who chose courage and justice over cowardice."

TOMMY VEXT (INTERNATIONAL MULTIPLATINUM RECORDING ARTIST, VOCALIST)

"Life truly has no rehearsal and Ian has exhibited the vulnerability, accountability and passion necessary to make positive changes in his life and inspire others to do the same."

PHIL HEATH (7X MR. OLYMPIA, ENTREPRENEUR, SPEAKER)

Milton Keynes UK
Ingram Content Group UK Ltd.
UKHW012018170823
427026UK00004B/304